W9-AHE-083

TOO MUCH IS NEVER ENOUGH

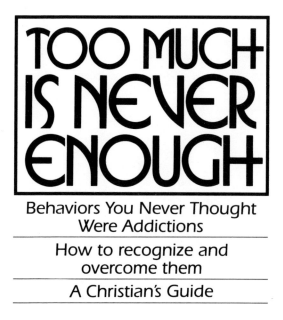

TOO MUCH IS NEVER ENOUGH

Behaviors You Never Thought
Were Addictions

How to recognize and
overcome them

A Christian's Guide

GAYLEN LARSON
WITH
MARITA LITTAUER

Pacific Press Publishing Association
Boise, Idaho
Oshawa, Ontario, Canada

Edited by Marvin Moore
Designed by Tim Larson
Cover photo by André Gallant/The Image Bank®
Typeset in 10/12 Janson

Library of Congress Cataloging-in-Publication Data:
Larson, Gaylen, 1947-
   Too much is never enough: behaviors you never thought were ad-
dictions: how to recognize and overcome them: a Christian's guide /
Gaylen Larson with Marita Littauer.
       p.   cm.
   ISBN 0-8163-1109-9
   1. Compulsive behavior—Religious aspects—Christianity. 2.
Christian life—1960- 3. Habit breaking—Religious aspects—Chris-
tianity. I. Littauer, Marita. II. Title.
BV4509.5.L37   1992
248.8'6—dc20   92-5729
                                                      CIP

92 93 94 95 96 ● 5 4 3 2

Contents

PART I

DISCOVERY

Introduction

Life is filled with good things, but many of us have too much of a good thing. "If a little is good, more must be better," they say—but is it?

Your life may be full of good things. You may go to choir practice on Monday night, Bible study on Tuesday night, prayer meeting on Wednesday night, and youth group on Thursday night. Your weekend may be filled with men's groups, women's groups, witnessing groups, and, of course, church. All wonderful things. But can you have too much of a good thing?

You may work very hard. You stay at the office late or bring work home almost every night. You haven't had a vacation in years, and most weekends find you spending at least half a day at the office. You've done well and your labors have been rewarded—you've had several promotions in the last few years. What's more, you live in the right house on the best side of town, and your children are assured of the best education possible. Work is a good thing. Something to be proud of. But is it possible to have so much that you'll never have enough?

Maybe when you got married you lived in a humble little apartment. You dreamed of owning a house and thought, "If we just had a little house with a yard and some flowers, we could be happy." Fifteen years later, you had the little house, but you needed a bigger one. You got the bigger one and upgraded it to a showplace, full of treasures found on European vacations. You also needed a motorhome to get away weekends. Every weekend you pack up and head off. You've toured the country and visited every beach. But that sedan you drive to work seems so basic. If you had a sports car, then you could be happy. Many people think that you have "too much," but for you, "too much is never enough."

Making supervisor was great. You were proud of your achievements, but then you had to make manager, and then it seemed that only the corner office could make you happy.

When you and your family first became Christians, the spiritual nourishment you found from worshiping with other believers seemed like an oasis in a difficult week. Soon you found that you needed to be with those people in that spiritual atmosphere more and more. "Too much was never enough." It's like the popular song by Madonna: "I'm so happy with what I've got, I want more."

Are you like that?

For you, it may not be church or religion or work or your lifestyle. Maybe you can't get enough exercise, sex, or sports. Or you need to shop, play with cars, or be with a certain person all the time. Many of us have something in our life that we think would make us happy if we could just get enough of it. What that "it" happens to be in your life isn't really important. What matters is the "why" and the "how."

- *Why* are you always reaching for more?
- *Why* don't you feel satisfied?
- *Why* aren't you happy?
- *How* did you get this way?
- *How* did you lose control?
- *How* are you going to get over it?

Recently I was at a party. A mother of three teenage girls told me that her high-school-age daughter had decided not to drink. The parents had offered to pay her car insurance if she agreed not to drink while she was in her teen years.

The mother said that the year before, when her daughter attended gatherings with her friends, they would call her Prissy Chrissy and tease her about being a Puritan. This year those same friends told her they wished they had her courage. They wished they could attend a party, have a good time, and not drink.

"Just say No," the girl told her friends, but they couldn't. It felt too good. They needed it.

What is going on in the life of sixteen- or seventeen-year-olds that makes them need a drink? What is so bad in their lives that they need to drink to feel good? Why do they live for the weekend? Why does it seem that they can't party enough?

What about your own life? You probably don't spend Saturday nights getting drunk at parties with loud music and inappropriate behavior, but what makes you feel good? Is there something you need? Is there something in your life that you can never get enough of?

In the following pages you will learn to identify what is known as addiction, especially psychological addiction. Most people associate the word *addiction* with a chemical that the human body comes to depend on for survival. But unlike an addiction to drugs, alcohol, smoking, etc., a psychological addiction doesn't involve a chemical that is taken internally. Psychological addictions involve an external person or activity that becomes necessary for survival. The psychological addict is mentally and emotionally dependent, and just as much a slave to his or her "drug of choice" as the chemical addict.

In this book you will discover the "whys" in your own life. Tests, definitions, examples, and guidelines will help you look at yourself and examine your past behaviors. When you are through, you will have a better understanding of the person you are today.

You will also learn the "hows"—practical things you can do right away to tell whether you have addictive tendencies. If you discover that you do, you will learn to pinpoint the exact areas of your life where these addictions exist. You'll learn how to overcome your addictions and what to expect in the process of recovery.

Most important, you'll learn to be happy with who you are without always striving for more. They say that "you can never be too rich or too thin," but it is possible to have too much of a good thing.

Chapter 1

What Is Addiction?

It is easy to point a finger at the teenager who is wasting his life away on drugs and say, "He has a problem with addiction." To the father who has to stop at the local bar for a few drinks before he can come home and face that teenager, it is easy to say, "He's addicted." The mother, facing the stress of her dysfunctional family, smokes a cigarette for relief and relaxation. When the pressure is on, she finds herself nervously smoking one after another. It is easy to say, "She has an addiction. She needs help."

Drugs, alcohol, and cigarettes are addictions. We all know that; a lot has been said about them. Books have been written, speeches have been given, and councils have been formed to help people cope with their addiction to drugs, alcohol, and cigarettes.

But what about the woman whose husband has left her? Her home is empty and lonely, and dealing with the rejection is too much for her to face. Each day she comes home from work dreading another evening in her empty house. After a hard day at work she thinks, "I deserve some ice cream. No one cares how I look anyway." So she stops and picks up a quart of Häagen-Dazs, adds some new cookies that she sees on sale, and heads home to nurse her wounds. The ice cream tastes good, and the cookies seem to round out the treat. After all, she deserves it. A few days later she's had another hard day. She deserves another treat. Maybe it's cake, maybe it's steak, but food becomes a way of coping.

Can eating be an addiction?

Or what about the woman who is struggling with a low self-esteem and feels that she is worthless? She just found out that God loves her and sent His Son to die just for her. It makes her feel so special. She wants to know more about this God. When the weekly Bible study starts, she never misses a week. Life at home is so miserable that she can barely make it through the week, but while worshiping with other Christians she feels her faith renewed, so she attends the Wednesday-night service and sings the praise songs with great conviction. She is invited to join the women's retreat committee and is put in charge of the mother-daughter banquet. The committee meetings are endless, but she sees her service to God as worth it all. Her kids complain that she's never home anymore, and they are tired of church potluck suppers, but she feels so much better at church that she keeps showing up at every opportunity.

Can church be an addiction?

Then there's the man whose job is totally unrewarding because his boss harps on him all day. Each morning he can scarcely drag his body out of bed. He moans, groans, pulls the pillow over his head, and vows that he's not getting up. His wife, who has already been up for hours, reminds him of the bills that are mounting and tells him he'd better get out of bed, get to work, and make something of himself. Staring in the mirror as he shaves, he dreams of the weekend, when he can bury his head in the pillow and sleep until he's ready to get up.

When he does get up on the weekend, out in the garage is the joy of his life: A classic car. His father's first car. He found it in the barn at his grandparents' home many years ago. It was rusty and dusty, and when he showed an interest in it, his father gave it to him. He brought it home on a trailer. He's sanded and pounded, painted and polished. The car has won many awards, and he's the hit of his car club.

He has a little picture of his wife and kids on his desk at work, but on the walls are plaques and pictures of his prize winner. On the days when there's a car show he bounds out of bed with great energy and enthusiasm. Recently he bought another old car. Some of the thrill is gone from his father's old car—after all, it's perfect now. The new one renews his purpose for living.

Can a hobby be an addiction?

It is said that a woman's place is in the malls. But when does enough shopping become too much? The average person visits a mall perhaps twice a month, but some people make it a daily routine. A woman whose husband is having an affair with a younger woman heads off to find herself some new clothes to attract him back. Armed with his credit cards she buys several cute new outfits. She feels younger and prettier. Surely he'll notice her now. Her friends like her new look, and her boss comments on how pretty she is, but at dinner her husband scarcely notices that she exists and leaves quickly, explaining that he needs to go back to the office to finish that big project.

Home alone, she packs up and heads for the mall. If she tries harder, maybe he'll notice. She buys some new dresses and gets her hair done. She keeps this up for several weeks, and her friends give her more compliments. She's feeling better all the time.

But soon the bills come in, and her husband has a fit. She feels hurt and wounded. The next day after work she goes shopping again. A pretty new dress will make her feel a lot better.

Can shopping be an addiction?

Christians may feel virtuous because they avoid all of those vices that enslave alcoholics and drug addicts, yet they may be just as addicted. The Christian's addiction may be more acceptable, but the disease is just as real and just as destructive to his or her emotional and spiritual life as alcohol or cocaine.

An addiction is the condition of being a slave to a habit or behavior. The addict is controlled by some desire or influence. A person who is addicted gives up his ability to choose. His desires force him to make choices that his logical mind knows are hurtful to his health or relationships.

Many programs have been developed to treat addictions to alcohol, tobacco, and narcotics. I am not attempting to rehash these well-covered topics. I do hope to open your eyes to areas in your lifestyle or the lifestyle of a loved one that may need some attention. An addiction in one part of life is a warning sign that some other part of life is out of line.

In his popular book, *Bradshaw: On the Family,* John Bradshaw says that a person is addicted when he or she "has a pathological relationship with a mood altering chemical." While mood-altering chemicals are certainly addictive, I have found that a mood-altering relationship or activity can be just as addictive.

Anything that alters a person's mood has the potential for turning into an addiction. People often become addicted to things that in small doses are positive and helpful. But when the activity or relationship becomes mood altering, and when it is used as a mechanism for coping, it has the potential of becoming an addiction.

Cindy came to our office seeking a cure for her loss of interest in life. She had an overwhelming depression, and although she was an attractive young woman in her early twenties, she couldn't seem to get herself going each day. She sold software for a prominent manufacturer, and her work offered many rewards and a lot of opportunity for advancement. When she first took the job, she felt excited. She looked forward to the challenges that her job offered.

Like many young women, Cindy felt concerned about her figure, so she joined a local gym. She was committed to staying in shape, because she did not want to end up looking like her mother or her older sister. She worked out every day, getting up early to start her day with a workout. The exercise increased her energy, and after a shower she felt better equipped to face the day. She began winning her company's monthly achievement awards and was heading for sales representative of the year.

With the increased thrill of winning and the "high" that she felt from her exercise, Cindy's daily routine advanced from an hour at the gym in the morning to another hour before supper "to work off the stress of the day." However, as her body adjusted to the increased workout, she had to put in even more hours to feel the same "rush" that she used to get from a single hour. Before long she was working out three to five hours a day, to the exclusion of all other activities in her life except her job. She became obsessed and focused her life totally on the "adrenalin rush" she got from muscle toning. When she worked out, Cindy tried to find a spot near the mirrors so she could watch her body performing better and better.

As a result, she withdrew from social activities, and both her personal and professional life began to suffer. Cindy didn't see what she was doing to herself, and the drop in her job performance made her work out even more. The cycle came to an abrupt halt when she pulled a muscle in her leg. Her doctor's orders seemed like the end of the world: "No exercise for six months!"

When Cindy came to me, all she knew was that she felt depressed and she was in trouble at work. Her depression had caused her employer to put her on probation, and she feared that she was close to losing her job. As we pieced together the puzzle, she began to see her pattern of addiction. She had always struggled with the question of

"Who am I?" When she worked out, she felt like she was finding the answer. At the gym she was part of a group. Life seemed worth living. It made her feel complete.

But the adrenalin fix that the exercise gave her turned her desire for fitness into an addiction. What she interpreted as an opportunity to be part of a group really cut her off from everything that was important to her. She was fortunate that her exercise addiction finally gave her a painful limp that forced her to look at the real issues in her life.

From my experience as a therapist, it is clear that many of us have the potential to form an addiction. The danger arises anytime we attempt to fill a void in our lives with some other relationship or activity instead of dealing with the void itself and the reasons why it exists. An outsider looking in may think that addictions are just the latest in the psychology craze. While there is an increase in the number of addictions, the increase is not just because of recent attention. Addictions have been around for a long, long time.

A quick look at our country's history reveals how America became an addicted society. Sixty years ago we had the Great Depression. At that time, people's attention was focused strictly on where the next meal would come from and how they would pay the rent. There was no time for exercising. There was no money for shopping at the mall or supporting a food addiction. More important, few of us had the mental time to spend looking at our emotional needs. The Depression ended as our country entered full force into World War II, but again we were distracted.

Only after the war ended did we get into trouble. The fifties, sixties, and seventies became the era of affluence. We actually had time to play and enjoy ourselves. With the luxury of our physical needs being met, we began to focus on our emotional needs, and often we did not like what we found. The fifties and early sixties were "party time." In the later sixties and seventies, having met our need for materialism, we began using mood-altering substances and activities. Drugs came into demand, and the results escalated.

The physical luxury that people in the Western world enjoy is unique in its psychological addictive capacity. The people in Third World countries spend much more of their time supplying the basic needs of life, and emotional needs take a back seat. These people appear to not have the addictive struggles that our society has to cope with.

We have allowed ourselves to become an addicted society.

Chapter 2

When Does Addiction Become Sin?

Evangelical Christians tend to have a rather simplistic attitude toward addiction. We know that acceptance or rejection of Jesus Christ as Lord and Saviour is up to us—our choice—and we tend to think that every other area of our lives, including abusive behavior and addiction, is also a matter of choice.

The will is an important part of any addiction, to be sure. The alcoholic, for example, chooses to take that first drink. After that, however, comes a series of repetitive drinking behaviors that finally progress to the point that he has actually given up his own will. He is so controlled by his desires that he no longer has the ability to "just say No." He is no longer able to choose.

In Romans 1, Paul teaches very clearly that when we continue to sin and rebel against God and suppress the truth of God, we are given over to our sinful desires. We have enslaved ourselves to these desires, which have become addictions in our lives. I am illustrating this point with alcoholism, but I could as well be using any of the other addictions that I will address throughout this book.

The key issue in addiction is not our willingness to give up the addiction. The issue is rather our willingness to admit that we have no control and are powerless over this addiction. We must "let go and let God," if you will. By the time our drug of choice has evolved into a full-blown addiction, we have been repeating the behavior over and over to the point that it has become a habit. A habit is something we do without thinking, like turning on a light when we enter a room. An

17

addiction is a habit that has become so powerful we have lost control of it. It controls us.

Paul addresses the frustration of sinful habits: "What I want to do I do not do, but what I hate I do" (Romans 7:15, NIV). As we repeat the behavior and find pleasure in it, we become slaves to it. Over a period of time we give up our will to this new god. Peter teaches in 2 Peter 2:19 that "man is a slave to whatever has mastered him" (NIV). Paul tells us in Romans 6:16, "Don't you know that when you offer yourselves to someone to obey him as slaves, you are slaves to the one whom you obey?" (NIV). A slave does not have the choice to obey or not to obey. Likewise, when we become enslaved to a habit, we must admit that we have no choice. We must admit that we are powerless to handle that behavior. We are addicted.

However, we can admit our desire to let go of that addiction so God can redeem us. God created Adam and Eve in the Garden of Eden with a will, with the ability to choose whether to worship Him. He wants us to *choose* to communicate with Him. Therefore, we must, by an act of our will, admit to God our powerlessness and our need of a Saviour.

To redeem something means to buy it back, to set it free, to rescue it, to save it. That's why Jesus Christ is our Redeemer. He bought us back from sin, from the slavery of our addictions. He paid the price so that we might be set free. But we must, by an act of our will, accept His redemption. God will not violate our will and force us to accept Him and His redemption. John 8:36 says, "If the Son sets you free, you will be free indeed" (NIV).

Why do 80 percent of abused children become child abusers? Because as children they didn't have a choice in what was done to them. Their abuser was bigger and stronger and forced them to do things that they would not have chosen to do. Because that choice was taken away from them, they feel enslaved to whatever it is they were forced to do. They build up defenses and learn to believe lies about themselves and about the "safety" of the world they live in. Their perception is tainted because of this experience.

The age of accountability is a critical issue and needs to be addressed in understanding child abuse or molestation that later leads to addiction. Because this enslaving experience in many cases occurred before the age of accountability, the victim must first be redeemed, set free. Then the healing can begin. The healing must first take place in changed thinking, with a recognition of the lies the victim has learned to believe about himself or herself.

The child who is sexually molested feels extremely powerless. Because things were done to her physically that she did not want to have happen, she feels that she still cannot say No. She feels that she has no control over her life. The perpetrator was bigger than she, stronger than she; she was under his control. Therefore, she perceives the world to be an unsafe place to live, and she approaches life guardedly rather than in an open and trusting way.

This can often be the beginning of an obsessive/compulsive disorder. Because she feels powerless, out of control in one area of her life, she overdoes in another area. She feels like she has to control *something* in her life. She may become a compulsive eater because the one area of her life that she feels she has control over is food. She didn't have control as a child with a dominating, abusive father, so she attempts to feel a sense of control by controlling her food. She can eat what she wants, when she wants. The issue is control.

You may remember the television special on the life of the popular songwriter Karen Carpenter. Her overcontrolling mother propelled her and her brother Richard into stardom. Karen starved herself to death at the height of her career. Her fans were shocked when the cause of her death was revealed: She had become anorexic. Her food and eating habits were the one area she could control.

A sexually molested child may perceive a secondary gain. Consciously or unconsciously, she feels that "if I'm fat, men won't pay attention to me, and I'll be safe. I won't be molested sexually again." Thus, her eating accomplishes two important things for her: control and safety.

The compulsive cleaner feels safe and acceptable because she is in control of her environment. She may clean the baseboards in her house every day; she will have the cleanest house in town. Her compulsive behavior has thrown other areas of her life totally out of balance, but because she's "in control" of her environment, she feels in control of her life. This is why she must have such a clean house.

The compulsive shopper feels like she has to shop. Her bumper sticker reads, "Shop till you drop." Shopping shields her from the hurts of her past. She has been wounded in one or more ways, sexually, perhaps, or through emotional or physical abuse. Her shopping, especially for clothes, makes her feel good about herself. "I'm not bad or dirty. See, I look good in the mirror. I'm OK. I can accept myself." It's her way of trying not to believe the lie that she unconsciously believes about herself—a lie that was taught her well before she reached the age of accountability.

Because the compulsive behavior accomplishes something "beneficial" within the addict, he or she continues to repeat it until it becomes an addiction. The very thing that at first she felt gave her control now controls her, and she realizes she can't say No. Recognizing her inability to control this part of her life, she compensates by becoming even more strong willed in order to compensate for the terrible things that happened to her in her childhood.

The healing process actually involves becoming less "strong willed," because the person who is not an addict has less need to compensate. Because she has less need to compensate, she has less need to practice her compulsive behavior. Healing has taken place through giving her need to control to the Lord. Thus, helping people become less willful is a major theme of the healing process, because the addict's willfulness is a direct response to the abuse she experienced as a child.

Most churches tend to look up to those who are successful leaders. She may be, for example, president of the women's organization. She may also be involved as a teacher in the children's class. She's there every single day that the doors are open. The best description of this woman is work, work, work. But if she is out of balance in other areas of her life, such as her relationships with her family and friends, then her work at church is probably an addiction. She's just as much out of balance, just as addicted, as the alcoholic or drug abuser.

It's the same with the businessman who gets overinvolved in jogging. When he jogs, he feels better about himself, he loses weight, and he gets a lot of compliments because of his physical shape. He has a higher energy level. As he runs, his endorphins kick in, and he gets "runner's high," so he runs farther and farther.

Dr. John Masten, professor at San Diego State University, states that 77 percent of long-distance runners experience this second wind. It fits a perfect pattern of our definition of addiction: mood alteration combined with repetition, which results in distraction. It's only a matter of time, as he keeps progressing in this newfound activity, till family, friends, work—in short, everything—will take second place. His life will be out of balance when it comes to running.

Addiction begins when a person comes to the point that he can't say No. When we are under stress and turn to our chosen behavior instead of turning to the Lord for a release of our stress, we are addicted. When the runner is under pressure, instead of turning to the Lord for strength through Bible reading, meditation, and prayer, he decides to run. This is why addiction can be called idolatry. The addict is worshiping at the altar of his addiction, because that is where he searches for strength rather than coming to Jesus. Whenever we place anything between us and God, we are committing idolatry.

One of our clients at the Alpha Counseling Program was clearly addicted to prayer. Prayer is very good. It is important to us as evangelical Christians. This woman, however, used prayer as a defense against other issues in her life. At home, when people in the family were doing something she didn't like, she would run away to her room and pray. No one, of course, would fault her for praying. The problem was that she was using prayer as a way to avoid dealing with the dysfunctional relationships in her life. It was her way of running away, her escape. A person is not necessarily superspiritual just because he or she exhibits behaviors that we normally interpret as spiritual.

I remember the case of a man in his late twenties who was married and had two small children. He claimed that he couldn't work because he was called to preach. His idea of preaching was to go around talking to people on the block, giving out tracts, and sitting by the seaside, enjoying God's creation. It might be easy, on the surface, to suppose that this person was called to be a prophet and that everyone should support his "ministry." The truth is, he was so dysfunctional in all his relationships that his "call to preaching" was nothing more than running away from life, trying to get good Christians to support him financially in his dysfunctional relationships. Everything else about his life was out of balance.

The pastor of a small congregation was addicted to preaching. It built his self-esteem. He used it to deal with his anger. He could pound on the pulpit and march around in front of everybody. They all interpreted this as very spiritual, but in reality this was his way of covering up his emotional shortcomings. Because he always felt better after expending his anger like this, he kept doing it over and over. He had become addicted to preaching.

Our fight is not against "flesh and blood" but against "principalities and powers of the spiritual realm" (see Ephesians 6:12). Our adversary, the devil, is "as a roaring lion . . . seeking whom he may devour" (1 Peter 5:8, KJV); he knows our weakness and will do all he can to destroy us.

In any addiction, there is a tremendous amount of self-deception. We believe lies about ourselves and the world we live in. Our adversary, the "father of lies," will do all he can do to destroy us, to trip us up. We must not be deceived as Adam and Eve were in the Garden of Eden. We must always be alert and aware because our enemy knows our weakness and will use every opportunity to attempt to use that weakness to destroy us.

The title of this chapter is, "When Does Addiction Become Sin?" Perhaps you wonder whether I have answered that question yet. No, I haven't. But I have given you the background that I think you need to understand the answer.

It's difficult to label an addiction sin when the behavior itself is good under normal circumstances. How can you say that the woman who prays constantly is sinning? Or that the man who works long hours at the office is sinning? Or that the girl who exercises three to five hours a day is sinning?

The problem is not with the behavior but with the imbalance in the behavior. Certain addictions are out-and-out sinful, such as adultery, incest, and the use of chemicals such as alcohol, tobacco, and narcotics that destroy the body, which is the temple of the Holy Spirit.

However, behaviors that are normal in themselves, but which we carry to excess because of the emotional relief they provide from other problems in our lives, are not sinful in quite the same sense. I prefer to think of these conditions as a result of the sinful environment in which we live, a result of the sinful nature that we all share because of the fallenness of the human race. As Christians, we should make every effort to overcome these addictions because they do affect our relationship with God. Anything that adversely affects our relationship with God becomes an idol if we refuse to deal with it, and idolatry is a sin.

Chapter 3

To What Do People Get Addicted?

From the story of Abraham and his son Isaac we learn that God wants nothing to come between us and our relationship with Him. Addictions are one of the things that can get in the way of our relationship with God and, as I mentioned in the previous chapter, anything that damages our relationship with God is wrong. Any habit that comes between us and God inhibits our spiritual growth, in addition to its cost to our physical and emotional health.

Since addiction creates a block between us and God, hindering our ability to communicate with Him, we must face the addictions in our own lives. If we are to live a spiritual, God-centered life, He must be the primary focus of all we do. But when we are addicted, the addiction becomes the primary focus.

Addictions come in many forms. People who face a daily struggle with socially unacceptable chemical addictions such as drugs, smoking, and drinking usually know that they are addicted. Most of us sitting in the average church pew don't have to deal with these obvious issues, and we may erase from our minds any idea that we might be addicted. But even though we are not chemically addicted, we may be just as addicted as those who drink, smoke, and use drugs.

Let me emphasize again that there are many good things that in small doses are good for a person. These areas are a cause for concern when they become a way to escape from life's problems, or a primary coping mechanism, to avoid dealing with the real issues. Any substance or repeated gratification that alters our mood has the potential to

23

become an addiction.

I have already mentioned church activities and spiritual exercises as potential addictive agents. I have also mentioned hobbies and exercise. These are addictive when they become a smoke screen that covers up the pain and emptiness we are feeling.

Another common addiction today is television. It is so easy to escape into the glamorous lives of the soap-opera characters. It is not uncommon to hear of people going through a major depression when a certain character is written out of a script. The character in the show dies, and the addicted viewer feels as though she has died too. She actually "grieves" the loss.

Mood-altering music has become very popular today. Its tranquil sounds soothe our fractured spirits, or we rap to its rhythm to get us going. Even praise music can alter our mood from sad to glad. While music is good, it can become an addiction. Some people can't sleep without soothing music to drown out the reality of life. It has become a habit. It has become an addiction.

Even a relationship with another person can be addictive. Most of us have a friend or two whom we can call when we are having a rough time. Those friends will let us dump all our problems on them, and when we are through, they can perk us right up. As the saying goes, "That's what friends are for." We all need friends. God planned it that way. The relationship becomes a concern when we need to talk to that person every day, and without him or her we can't seem to get moving. Addiction to a person can be either someone outside the family who is a friend, or it can be a spouse.

Some men may think they'd like a wife who is addicted to sex. God intended sex to be a beautiful relationship between a man and a woman, but it becomes a warped addiction when it is used to fill an unmet emotional need.

I remember John and Cindy. They couldn't understand why they weren't really happy in their marriage. They thought they were so perfectly matched to one another, and they really were in love. After all, they often had sex two or three times a day, and on weekends they spent hours in bed together. While good sex is often an indication of a healthy marriage, it takes more than good sex to make a healthy marriage. John and Cindy were both addicted to sex. Though in one sense it met a different need in each of their lives, it did do one thing for each of them: it filled a void.

Cindy never felt close to anyone while she was growing up, but she did not recognize this as a factor in her marriage. As a child, she knew that her mother loved her and that she was well provided for. When I asked her how she knew her mother loved her, Cindy responded with comments like, "She bought me nice clothes," or, "Mamma loves her baby," or, "We had a nice house." As Cindy and I progressed, we discovered that while her mother did undoubtedly love her, she never showed any form of physical affection. She never said, "Come sit on Mama's lap while I read you stories."

"Mom waved me off to bed each night," Cindy recalls, but her older brother was responsible for seeing that she got there. When Cindy came home from school each day, she wanted Mama to reach out and hug her, but all she ever got was, "How did school go today, honey?" Cindy would respond with a despondent "Fine" and go to her room to do her homework.

Cindy headed into her marriage with an unknown craving for physical affection. She was thrilled that John wanted to touch her. She loved being held. Because sex was the ultimate form of physical affection, she wanted it all the time!

John also wanted sex all the time, but his needs came from a different source. His father beat him whenever he didn't measure up to his father's unattainable standard. If John responded to his father's abuse with anger—the natural response—his father would beat him again. John was not allowed to express his feelings, and as he headed into his teenage years he was an angry, bitter young man who was filled with an internal rage. He did, however, discover a way to cope. A friend showed him how to masturbate. For the first time in his life he felt a release from the pent-up anger. When he and Cindy got married, he still carried around his childhood anger, and almost any small event would set him off. He wanted sex two or three times each day. Sex was his form of release. It was his addiction.

John and Cindy were both using sex to fill needs in their lives. Sex was a substitute. It filled Cindy's need for security and physical affection. It provided a way for John to deal with his anger. Neither of them was facing the real issues in their lives, and as a result, each one needed more and more sex in order to cope. But it was like trying to fill the Grand Canyon with a hand shovel. They were spending all their free time trying to fill these individual needs. Yet the problems remained, and, predictably, the marriage relationship apart from sex was struggling. Sex was only a temporary anesthetic.

John and Cindy's case may sound extreme, but while the names may change and the facts will vary, many people have a sexual addiction. Dr. Arnold Washton, director of the Washington Institute on Addictions in New York, states that "for sex addicts, sex is the drug that is used in a never-ending search for relief, distraction, comfort, excitement, and a sense of power or other effect having little to do with the sex itself."

Another addictive behavior is workaholism. We all need to work, but some people use work to deal with their feelings of inadequacy. We need to be concerned when work becomes an all-consuming passion to the exclusion of other activities and relationships.

Hershel came for counseling after his wife threatened to leave him if he didn't get help. He couldn't understand her concern. They lived on the right side of town, drove the right cars, and their children went to the right private schools. Hershel's employees praised him, as did his competitors. His plumbing-supply business had become the largest in the region and was known throughout the country. But his wife Lee complained that he was never home. She became particularly upset when he was on a business trip during their son's graduation. Now he was in my office.

Hershel had set out to build an empire. He wanted it to be so big that people from all over would praise him and come to study his technique. Surely his father would notice him then. As a little boy his father had told him, "You'll never amount to anything. Why can't you be more like your older brother?" His father created feelings of inferiority that became deeply imbedded in Hershel's mind. It took weeks of discussion for him to see that never-ending work was an attempt to gain his father's approval. He had gotten the praise of his brothers and his mother. One of his older brothers even worked for him, but his father never said, "You've done well, son. I'm proud of you."

Three years ago, Hershel's father died. Hershel never heard the words he needed from his father. Without realizing it, he was still working hard to win his father's approval, which was now unobtainable. His father had created a black hole that Hershel could never fill, no matter how hard he worked. He was on a journey to fill the emptiness and pain that was caused by his father's rejection. Hershel began to heal when he recognized that he had a problem and understood where it came from.

What about you? You may not be addicted to the things we typically think of as addictions—drugs, alcohol, or cigarettes. But what about the normal things that we don't usually think of as addictions? Could something be holding you as a slave? Are you addicted to church activities, a hobby, exercise, shopping, TV, music, relationships, sex, or work? The object of your compulsive behavior is not as important as the reason why you are addicted to it.

Remember, anything is an addiction when it provides an escape from the real problems in your life and when you have to have it in order for life to even go on.

Chapter 4

Why Do Some People Get Addicted and Others Don't?

Suzie's life was a mess. Her husband had left her a few months before she came into our office. It wasn't his departure that had her in such a suicidal state. That was just the icing on the cake. The real trouble was that she couldn't face her own problems. One day she heard one of our therapists on a radio program and decided to call our hot-line number. The counselor who answered her call calmed her down and convinced her not to take her life. Now she was in our office to sort out the pieces and try to put them back together.

Suzie's mom and dad had divorced when she was three years old. Her dad came to pick her up occasionally, but the visits became more and more infrequent. Suzie felt like the divorce was her fault, and she was sure her dad didn't love her.

Her mom remarried when she was five, and for a while, life got a lot better. Mom didn't have to work anymore, and she was able to stay home with Suzie. Her stepfather had three children who were all older than she, and they moved in when "Dad" did. For the first time Suzie had siblings—all boys. But Mom's attention was now divided, and Suzie began questioning her mom's love for her. Because Suzie's mom was afraid of disrupting the new family, she nearly always sided with the other children.

Suzie's mom and stepfather went out a lot at night, leaving Suzie with her brothers. When the cats were away, the mice began to play, and Suzie became the center of sexual games. She hated what they made her do, but they threatened to tell her mom that

28

she had been a bad girl if she didn't participate. She knew if she told her mom she'd be sent to her room and have her toys taken away, so she cooperated.

As Suzie grew up she had a great vacuum inside her. She longed to be loved and to feel special. Sex became such a part of her life that in later years, whenever boys approached her in school she was an easy target. She was so starved for love that she went out with any boy who asked her and did whatever he wanted, hoping he wouldn't leave her. When she finally got married, she doted on her husband and did everything she could think of to please him. At work she flirted with the men in her office in an attempt to get the love she still craved.

But the emptiness she felt for love couldn't be filled with these things, and she bounced back and forth between addictions. She'd drink, she'd shop, and she'd sleep around. Now her husband had left her, and she was more desperate than ever for love and attention. She took whatever she could get, and it wasn't good.

Judy lived in the same town and had attended the same high school at the same time as Suzie. Her parents also got divorced when she was young. Because she thought it was her fault, she felt rejected. When Judy was in the seventh grade, one of her teachers molested her.

Like Suzie, Judy came from a divorced home, which left her feeling rejected. And, like Suzie, Judy was sexually abused. But today Judy's life is quite normal. She is married, and she and her husband have a fairly good relationship. She has struggled with sex, but her husband has been helping her to deal with the problem.

How could two girls from the same town, who attended the same school at the same time and had virtually the same problems, end up so differently? Why do some people get addicted and others don't?

Many factors go into making an addiction. With the right (or wrong) combination of factors, an addiction to one or more things is likely to result. Unless a person realizes where he's heading and gets help to work through the unprocessed pain that is propelling him into his compulsive behavior, an addiction is almost inevitable.

If you watch TV, listen to the news, or read the newspaper, you will hear about research that is being done on addiction. Much of the emerging medical evidence shows that some people are born with a chemical imbalance which makes them more susceptible to addiction than others. While the imbalance is different in different people, the result is the same.[1] The mind and body are unable to function at their best. For example, the adult children of alcoholics are two to four times more likely to choose alcohol as an escape and become alcoholics themselves than the rest of the population. The adult child of an alcoholic may choose alcohol because he inherited that tendency or because he may have had poor parenting. Whatever the cause, as a child he learned from his parents that drinking was an effective and acceptable way to deal with stress.

In their book *Craving for Ecstasy,* authors Harvey Milkman and Stanley Sunderwirth do an excellent job of showing that the predisposition to alcohol may be present in the neurotransmitters of the brain. However, they also show that other factors are needed in order for a person to become an alcoholic. All who struggle with addictions have the common ingredient of low self-esteem or a feeling of worthlessness. Even people who have a physiological predisposition to addiction to alcohol are not likely to become alcoholics unless low self-esteem is also part of their personality mix.

The problem with saying that alcoholism or any other addiction is solely a genetic or medical issue is that it relieves the addict of the responsibility for his or her own actions. If we treat an addiction strictly as a medical problem, we treat it with medication. This tends to delay the need to deal with the root cause of the addiction. In the twenty years that I have been working with people who suffer from addictions, I have found that the cause goes deeper than what it appears to be on the surface. Rarely if ever is the problem solely a chemical imbalance.

Another reason for a predisposition to addiction is the addict's own personality, how he deals with stress in his life. The strongly driven, choleric personality is often a workaholic. Rather than talking about the problems in his life, he deals with his stress through aggressive behavior and is likely to fall into addictions such as work, sports, or exercise.

The insider-trading scandals of the eighties revealed many such personalities. Dennis Levine was one of the first to fall. After several

---

1. I'm not talking about people who are born addicted to drugs because their mother continued to use drugs heavily while she was carrying them.

years in prison, he told his story to *Fortune* magazine. He said, "I thrive on stress." This is typical of someone with his type of personality. As he looked at his past he explained, "At the root of my compulsive trading was an inability to set limits. Perhaps it is worth noting that my legitimate success stemmed from the same root. My ambition was so strong it went beyond rationality, and I gradually lost sight of what constitutes ethical behavior. At each new level of success I set higher goals, imprisoning myself in a cycle from which I saw no escape. When I became a senior vice president, I wanted to be a managing director, and when I became a managing director, I wanted to be a client. If I was making $100,000 a year, I thought, *I can make $200,000*. And if I made $1 million, *I can make $3 million*. And so it went."

Dennis didn't talk with anyone about his problems. Even his wife Laurie had no idea of the illegal activities he had succumbed to. He admits, "By the time I made partner at Drexel, I was out of control."

The person with a naturally shy or quiet disposition—the phlegmatic—also tends to hold his problems inside rather than reaching out for help. There may be people in his circle of friends and relatives who would be more than willing to help, but his natural response is to hold the problems inside and try to deal with them on his own. This personality type is afraid to deal with conflict, but he can't hold his feelings inside forever, so he finds other ways to cope with the struggles we all face in life. The need for coping pushes the quiet person into addictive behavior.

Walt was raised by a very strong-minded father who became a powerful authority figure. His father was a firm believer in the axiom that children are to be seen and not heard. At a very early age little Walter learned not to express his feelings or emotions. He just held them inside. No one knew what he was really feeling. When he tried to express his feelings, his father shot him down by saying things like, "Big boys don't cry," "Be a tough guy," or, "Don't be a wimp."

Any time Walt was in conflict with his father and tried to express how he felt, he always lost. When his mother and father had a disagreement, his mother always lost. Dad was bigger and emotionally stronger, and he'd slap Walt's mother a few times until she gave in. Walt's father wanted everyone to know that he was the man of the house. His size and power dominated the family, and he made sure that he won every dispute.

Junior high school was a critical time for Walt. He wasn't the life-of-the-party type, and his home life kept him emotionally stunted. His domineering father kept him from expressing any of his feelings of inadequacy or the rage building up inside. In high school, and later, college, he compensated for his insecurity by studying hard and getting good grades. He was an academic success, but inside he still harbored all those feelings of inadequacy and anger. Any time he felt uptight, he would follow his learned behavior from childhood and hold it all inside. He refused to face the least potential conflict because he had learned that he would lose, so why try?

Shortly after college Walt got married, and with his wife's family, for the first time, he began to feel like he belonged in a man's world. His new male relatives were avid sports fans who spent hours watching sports events on TV, and Walt, anxious for acceptance, joined them. He had never been good at sports himself, which put him at a bit of a disadvantage in gaining the friendship of the average man. But now he didn't have to participate in sports to be accepted. He had the fellowship of other men by watching the events on television with them.

Whenever he watched a ballgame he felt an emotional release. He didn't understand what was taking place, but he knew that when the game was over and the guys went home, he felt better. He naturally wanted to keep that good feeling, so he searched the *TV Guide* to find the next sporting event that would give him an opportunity to have the guys over again. He mistakenly thought that these good feelings were coming from the fellowship with other men. This became so important that he purchased a big-screen TV, and to heighten the excitement he got a Surround Sound audio system. His family couldn't really afford all that luxury, but he felt that it was a good investment.

There was another aspect to Walt's addiction. It's OK to have friends, but lack of friends wasn't the problem. The real problem was his suppressed anger, and for the first time in his life, he had found a way to express these feelings, to deal with his pent-up rage. If he thought a play was called unfairly, he would jump up and down and scream at the TV. The TV didn't fight back, and he felt like he'd won even if the call wasn't changed by his antics.

At first, watching sports seemed to be his "salvation." He always felt better after a good game. In the past a conflict had always thrown him into a depression, but sports gave him a release, and he felt better. His mood was altered. In itself, this was OK. The problem came when this good outlet began to dominate his life. His wife and children were unhappy because they felt left out. He coped with this conflict by watching more sports. This gave him more safe things to yell at, which released the anger he felt. As time went on, TV sports dominated more and more of his life, until eventually they evolved into a full-fledged addiction. The goal, of course, is to deal with the root cause so that addiction is not needed.

Someone with an introverted personality like Walt, when combined with a dysfunctional family, will almost surely develop an addiction. The addiction is an "acceptable" way to release pent-up emotions.

People with a low tolerance for pain often develop an addiction. I know two sisters, Martha and Louise. Martha has a high pain tolerance, while her sister Louise has a very low tolerance. Both come from the same family, but they deal with pain very differently. When Martha goes to the dentist, she asks how long the actual drilling will take. If it is under three minutes, she skips the Novocain and clasps her hands tightly together. Louise, on the other hand, has the dentist give her laughing gas so she won't feel the needle go in when the doctor gives her a Novocain shot! Martha deals with the pain, while Louise tries to escape it.

The same is true with mental and emotional pain. Someone with a low tolerance for emotional pain is more likely to become involved in addictive behavior. He or she is predisposed toward addictive behavior.

Priscilla had a low tolerance for emotional pain. She was the typical California "beach bunny." She was cute, young, blond, thin, and attractive. Her personality had a childlike quality, a certain naiveté. Priscilla sought out people who could take care of her. She always looked for a father figure in her boyfriends—someone who could meet all of her emotional needs. Priscilla was brought up in a Christian home and was active in her local church. She knew right from wrong. She knew what the Bible said about premarital sex, but in spite of her best intentions, she kept getting sexually involved. Yet she was afraid of the consequences and felt very frustrated.

Priscilla had a history of running away from emotional pain. As a child she learned to heal a hurt by doing things that felt good. Throughout college she was the life of the party. She would date constantly and keep herself in a whirlwind of activity. Instead of dealing with the pain of her low self-worth, she escaped it. Life felt better when she was having fun!

But "fun" has its down side too—a hollow, empty feeling. Nights were great, but when the sun came up and she was alone again, she felt used. Yet she continued choosing activities that covered up the pain, even if it was just for a while. Weekends she and her boyfriend would head off to some exciting place, but during the week she lived with guilt. The next weekend she covered up the pain with more sexual frivolity, and during the week she wallowed in guilt. It was a vicious cycle. She was caught in an addiction that covered up her pain.

Priscilla had never learned to grow emotionally. She was stuck in the mode of an eternal teenager. Party, party, party, with no sense of responsibility. The teenage struggles she had faced were normal enough for teenagers, but because of her low threshold for emotional pain she didn't grow through the problems. Growth is usually achieved through pain. In therapy we often say, "No one changes unless they are hurting." In Priscilla's case she covered her pain with social activity. Her fear of pain kept her from growing, causing her to regress into an addiction. Her childlike quality was "cute" to the men she dated, but it kept her trapped in an empty party life. She had become a "party addict."

It is possible to move beyond such pain and learn to deal with it constructively. Some time ago one of our therapists taught a natural childbirth class. We were connected with a local hospital that was looking for a couple of mothers who were willing to have their child's birth videotaped for use in future training. In exchange, the hospital agreed to waive all delivery charges. Two mothers volunteered.

When it came time for the births, the first mother prepared herself for the taping and positioned herself as gracefully as possible. As the cameras rolled, she began the breathing exercises she had been taught, smiled at the camera, and even waved from time to time. Twenty-five minutes later a beautiful baby was placed in her arms.

The other mother also prepared herself for the taping. She was positioned properly, had her glasses on, wore a fresh new bathrobe, and even had her hair fixed with a nice pink bow. But within five minutes she was sweating, her hair was a mess, her glasses were crooked, and she was screaming in pain. Out of all her agony, another beautiful baby was born.

The second mother obviously had a lower threshold of pain. It was no surprise to our therapist to learn that she was also a recovering cocaine addict. He admired her choice. She had made a major effort to face this delivery without her usual pattern of drowning the pain. Instead, she took responsibility for the pain and refused to lose herself to a mood-altering drug. By choosing to let the pain help her grow, she gave her child a healthier chance in life, and she also set in motion a change in her family dynamic. She broke the chain of escapism and fear and gave her child a chance to experience a drug-free life.

Childhood trauma, often called pain of the past, when left untreated, almost always sends its victim looking for a form of escape that results in an addiction. The trauma can be emotional, physical, or sexual. The results will be the same. Often childhood traumas befall those who have a genetic or chemical imbalance, an introverted personality, or a low threshold of pain. The various tendencies toward addictions become interwoven.

For example, we think of alcoholism as a genetic disease. It may be in some cases, but frequently it is not so much a genetic problem as it is a breakdown in the family system. If the father used alcohol to cope with his problems, his children are likely to adopt the same coping method and become alcoholics themselves. Furthermore, children who grow up in an alcoholic home usually suffer at least emotional abuse, if not physical or sexual abuse, which further increases the likelihood that they will cope the way they were taught—with alcohol.

The person who has a sweet and gentle personality is often sought out by a sexual perpetrator because she is easier to conquer and won't put up a fight. Personality and abuse are often linked together, and the combination pushes the victim into addictive behavior.

The person with a low tolerance for pain is often from a home that was filled with pain. He was an easy target for a domineering parent because he could be controlled so easily by being threatened with emotional pain. A person with a low pain threshold will absorb life's pain rather than fight it, and thus he needs to alter his mood to cope.

When abuse, whether emotional, physical, or sexual, is present alone or in combination with any of the other predispositions to addiction, the result will usually be an addiction or co-dependent relationship of some sort.

As a teenager I had a paper route, from which I "graduated" to a "real" job at a grocery store. I was proud to be a box boy at Pay-and-Take It. My job involved frequent trips to the parking lot each day. I would take the shoppers' bags outside and load them into their cars. I also gathered up all the shopping carts that had been left in the parking lot and brought them inside.

One sunny afternoon I was doing my usual routine, when I heard a strange noise. I looked around, and a few cars over I saw a man attacking a young woman. He was ramming her head into the front fender of what I assumed was their car.

As a sixteen-year-old who was just beginning to feel his man-hood, I thought that the only difference between me and Superman was a large *S* emblazoned on the chest. I rushed over to save the girl. "Let go of her!" I shouted. I expected it would be just like the movies. She would look adoringly at me and express her eternal gratitude that I had come to her rescue, and then she would sprint off into the distance.

The man did stop his attack momentarily, but you can imagine my surprise when the woman peeled herself away from the car and began swearing at me. She told me I shouldn't have interrupted them—that it was none of my business. Her words were venomous and laced with words that I had not heard in all my sixteen years. I'll never forget how I felt as I headed off to gather up the shopping carts. Why wasn't she pleased that I had saved her?

Since then I have learned a few things. An abuse victim will often develop an unusual addiction—the need to recreate her past. I later learned that this young woman had been repeatedly abused by her father. As a child she "knew" that Daddy loved her. To her, the abuse was Daddy's way of saying, "I love you." In her adult relationships she continually sought out men who were older than she, who had a need to control others. I later learned that the brute in the parking lot was seven years older than the woman—a father figure to her—and he abused her the same way her father had. To her, this meant she was loved. She had learned from childhood that abuse was better than no attention at all. Childhood abuse is one of the things that makes some people become addicts.

One person can attend church every week, and it's no problem at all. Another can attend just as regularly, and it becomes an addiction. For some people, a glass of wine at dinner is just a beverage. For others it's an addiction. The difference lies in each one's personal makeup. In his book *Bradshaw: On the Family*, John Bradshaw talks about the alcoholic. He says that a person is an alcoholic when his relationship with alcohol is more important than family, friends, and work. The relationship progresses to the point where alcohol is necessary to feel normal.

But the addiction doesn't have to be alcohol or some other mood-altering substance. It can be an activity or a relationship. A person should take action any time the thing or activity begins to adversely affect his or her normal life.

The book *God Help Me Stop*, written by an anonymous author, states, "Our compulsion-addiction is also a disease of the spirit. When we are in bondage to something of this world, we cannot at the same time love and serve God (Matthew 6:24). Therefore, our compulsion-addiction separates us from God." As Christians we must search our own lives for any patterns that make us predisposed to an addiction. We must remove anything that separates us from God.

Some people are definitely more likely candidates for addiction than others because they have a genetic predisposition or a chemical imbalance that begins the process. But in nearly every case there is also a personality problem that causes the individual to look for an escape rather than to deal with the problem at hand. And the result is always the same: behavior that is out of control—addiction.

Chapter 5

How Do Addictions Happen?

People don't go to bed one night happy, healthy, and well adjusted and wake up the next day addicted. An addiction develops gradually. It "grows on you." You work up to it. People use addictions to mask emotional pain in the present or to distract themselves from unprocessed pain in their past. Dr. Lawrence J. Hatterer, author of *The Pleasure Addicts*, states, "All addictions are developed as ways to handle anxiety, conflict and stress."

The pain in the present may be an unhappy marriage or an unfulfilling job, and people cope with it by developing an addiction that will distract their mind. Or their pain may be the result of some trauma in the past such as sexual abuse, rejection, abandonment, or the death of a parent or loved one. Many addictions actually begin in our parents. In Exodus 34:7 and Numbers 14:18, we read that the sins of the fathers are passed on to the third and fourth generations. Many refer to this as the "generational curse."

I have seen this Scripture passage fulfilled in the lives of many people with addictive behaviors, except that I would not say they are cursed. Rather, they are living out the coping patterns they learned through their parents' modeling. People learn to deal with problems the way their parents did. If your parents were alcoholics, the likelihood that you will become an alcoholic is 250 percent greater than someone whose parents were not alcoholics.

In trying to understand why people develop addictive behavior, we need to look at where the behavior originated. Stanton Peele, author of *Love and Addiction*, says that "when a person is strongly predisposed to be addicted, whatever he does can fit the psychological pattern of addiction. Unless he deals with his weaknesses, his major emotional involvements will be addictive, and his life will consist of a series of addictions."

Often the tendency to addiction will be the result of an early childhood trauma such as emotional or sexual abuse that the person cannot remember. A trained specialist can recognize many of the symptoms of childhood trauma, including addictive behaviors, but when the addict looks at his past, he cannot see it.

Jennifer is a good example. She came for counseling for her depression. A friend had encouraged her to get help. She was twenty-eight years old and quite attractive. She had been married to a successful man for four years and had no children. She found that she was often depressed and would eat to cheer herself up. Her eating caused a weight gain that depressed her even more, so she took diet pills and laxatives to lose weight. While she managed to keep her weight down, her health was in danger and her emotions were a mess. Jennifer thought that depression was her main problem.

In our initial conversation I asked Jennifer a variety of questions about herself, her personal values, and her childhood. She admitted to never feeling good about herself. She could see that her obsession to stay thin was motivated by a desire to boost her poor self-image, but she had no idea where the problem came from. When I asked if she had been sexually abused as a child, she snapped back with a firm No.

Jennifer came from a loving, closely knit family that went to church every Sunday. They were well cared for. Each Sunday Jennifer, her three sisters, and her little brother were dressed in good clothes, and the family went to church together. Her father was a good man, a deacon in their church, and a firm, though not abusive, disciplinarian. He had a soft voice and gentle manners. He was a large man who had brought his children up to honor their parents, and he maintained complete control over his family. From the outside theirs looked like the perfect Christian home.

However, Jennifer had been sexually abused, though she did not at first recognize the incestuous overtones in her relationship with her father. She thought that what had taken place in her bathroom was normal. This is often the case with sexual abuse victims. Jennifer never had sexual intercourse with her father. Rather, their home had an open-door policy—the doors to the bathrooms were never locked, and frequently they were not even closed.

When Jennifer started to develop into a young woman, her father started dropping in on her while she was bathing. He would lean against the sink and talk to her while she bathed. They discussed problems she was having in school or with boys, and he gave her advice on growing up. He helped her to dry off when she got out of the tub. He told her it was so nice they could have these private little chats to help prepare her for adult life.

Although she wasn't comfortable with his presence, she thought it was just a part of parenting, growing up, parents and children being open and honest with each other. When she was sixteen her father insisted that it was time she learn how to give herself an enema. He purchased the necessary supplies, locked the two of them in the bathroom, and told her how to proceed. Then he watched to be sure she did it right. Her bathroom time with her father continued until she got married at twenty-three. She even remembers how uncomfortable she felt the night before her wedding when her father was drying her off and giving her a final bit of advice.

Yet Jennifer thought this was normal—what all fathers did with their daughters. She thought there must be something wrong with her because she didn't like this "extra care." With these feelings of insecurity and sexual abuse in her background, Jennifer lived with daily depression and an addiction to food.

The depression was a result of her anger. People cannot be depressed and angry at the same time. Since she felt she could not be angry with her father—after all, he was only trying to help her grow up—she directed her anger back onto herself. The result was depression. Her eating disorder accomplished two things. First, it helped her feel good. Most of us learned during infancy that something in our mouth made us feel secure. Second, Jennifer learned that her overweight gave her sexual protection. As long as she was overweight, she was unattractive, and therefore undesirable, to men. She didn't feel feminine. She didn't feel sexual. She felt safe.

Many people who struggle with an addiction have a past that is checkered with sexual abuse, physical abuse, or some other form of deviant behavior, but they have no idea that what happened to them was wrong. They grew up with it, and it seemed normal. I recall one girl I talked with whose older brother had forced her to have oral sex with him, but she didn't see that as abuse because he had apologized and made her pray to ask God to forgive *her* for what *she* had done!

The following list will help you understand the bounds of normal behavior. Look it over, and see if you can determine how much of your past was normal.

Normal, Healthy Behaviors
- Physical affection such as basic hugging and kissing.
- Trust for each other.
- Open and honest communication.
- Privacy while bathing.
- Having fun together, enjoying each other's company.
- Sense of belonging.
- Sense of value to other family members.
- Home is comfortable, a place you go to feel safe.
- Sense that Mother and Father will take care of you.
- Face pain by showing honest hurt feelings with family members.

Unhealthy Family Behaviors
- French kissing or touching in sexual areas.
- Behavior such as keeping bedroom doors locked that shows family members don't trust each other.
- Only talking about superficial things. Feelings are not expressed. "Kids are to be seen and not heard." Dishonest communication.
- Father or other relatives watching while bathing or changing clothes.
- Avoiding each other, planning to stay away from home while other family members are home.
- No sense of belonging or closeness. Wishing you were part of someone else's family. No sense of value for each other.
- Avoiding being home because it feels uncomfortable or unsafe.
- Feeling responsible for your mother and father's happiness and well-being.
- Avoiding pain, covering it up with drugs, alcohol, anger, etc.

If you find that you, like Jennifer, have been struggling to cover up feelings that seem to have no source, but now you recognize an abnormal behavior in your past, you may be starting to understand the cause of your addiction. You will also have taken the first step in the healing process.[1]

However, the root of your addiction may be something recent and fresh that just got out of control. Alan experienced one stroke of bad luck after another. His father died when he was in high school. He got married young and had one child, but that relationship ended in divorce. He had just taken a promising new job with a telephone supply company when the company was bought out by a larger company, and his job was eliminated. Alan bounced around trying to find work in his field and ended up having to move to an unpopular place to get a job. One good thing happened in this new place, though. He had the chance to buy the classic Corvette he had always wanted.

He thought luck was really in his favor when he inherited a large sum of money from his grandfather. Now he could leave this awful place, go to the beach that he loved, and start his own telephone electronics business. But one year later he had used up all his grandfather's money and had to close his dream business.

Alan got a job with the city where he lived, but it paid less than he had been getting five years earlier, and it provided no opportunity for him to use either his education or his skills. At first Alan was thrilled to have found a job so quickly, but within a few months, he was bored, unchallenged, and depressed. He decided that he at least had a nice place to live—and he still had his Corvette. Yes, the Corvette!

For three years Alan lived for his car. He hated to get up each morning and head to his unfulfilling job, but he loved coming home at night. Each evening and every weekend found him working on his car. He redid the outside. He redid the inside. He fixed the wires and the engine. The car gave him the challenge and the creativity that he missed on the job. It gave him a purpose in life.

Alan could have become addicted to his car. Before it got to that point, though, he was able to change directions. He applied to law school. He really enjoyed the classes he had to take to prepare for his Law School Admission Test, and he liked the school environment.

---

1. Additional help for sexual abuse victims can be found in Fred and Florence Littauer's book, *Freeing Your Mind From Memories That Bind* and Fred Littauer's book *The Promise of Restoration: Breaking the Bonds of Emotional Bondage.*

Even though he didn't get accepted at the only university that he really wanted to attend, he learned one thing from the effort. He needed to get away from his present job and try something new. With all the problems in his past, Alan decided to get a master's degree in marriage and family counseling. He did well on his entrance exams and was accepted to the school of his choice.

At the time I am writing this book, Alan is doing well with his studies and learning a lot about himself. He's having a great time. For the first time in his life, Alan really loves what he's doing. His friends and family have commented on how great he looks and how much more fun he is to be with. The interesting thing is that his car hardly ever gets attention anymore. He still has it, and he plans on keeping it, but it is no longer the focus of his attention. Now, as a reward for his hard work, he takes it for a drive every now and then.

Addictions start with some pain or discomfort in life, and it doesn't really matter whether the pain is deep and unidentified or recent and easy to spot. The addiction begins when, instead of dealing with the problem, we try to escape it, to distract our minds from it, to cover it up. The pain gnaws away at our happiness, and we go in search of relief.

Any time we have emotional pain, we have two choices. We can either face it head on, get into counseling, and make changes in our lives the way Alan did, or we can run away the way Jennifer did. Repeated escaping usually leads to an addiction.

People get into addictive behavior to relieve the pain they feel, but it really becomes a cycle that adds to the pain. The addictive behavior, whether it is a substance, a behavior, or a relationship, becomes an anesthetic, and as with any anesthetic, the more you take, the more you need to dull the pain. At this point the anesthetic becomes an addiction. It takes over the victim's life and he becomes its slave. Everyone needs an escape from life's pressures from time to time. We should be concerned, however, about two developments: when we need our escape more and more often, and when it takes control of our life to the point that we can't say No.

People often become addicted to prescription drugs. It all starts innocently enough. Say you have trouble calming down or dropping off to sleep, and the doctor suggests a little tablet to help you out. If the tension is the result of a temporary crisis, you may use a few of the pills and put them away when the stress is over. But if the problem is deeper, either from buried trauma in the past or from an ongoing situation in the present, you will find the pills harder to put away. You will also find that continued relief requires more and more pills. Millions of Americans are addicted to Valium. They start with a little, maybe one a day when they are under extreme pressure. The medication loosens them up, and they feel so much better that they begin taking one every day all the time and two a day when they are under pressure. The cycle goes on like that until they are taking several a day, and they can't face the world without them.

Drugs also cause a physical addiction—the body begins to demand the chemical. Except for this physical demand, though, psychological addiction is the same as chemical addiction. If life deals yet another blow, coping requires even more of the anesthetic. An addiction becomes a vicious cycle that feeds itself. It masks one pain while creating another pain.

For example, the woman who grew up in an alcoholic home and never got the love and approval she needed heads into adult life longing for attention and self-worth. She discovers that shopping gives her a sense of value. When she buys pretty new clothes, people pay attention to her and compliment her. So the next time she's down she goes shopping and gets cheered up. This plan works fine until the bills come in. Then, in addition to relieving her pain, shopping has become a marriage problem that causes financial stress, which causes problems in her relationship with her husband. As the relationship at home deteriorates, she needs more relief, so she goes shopping again. Eventually she may have her credit cards taken away and her checking account closed, but the problem will remain and resurface as soon as the financial stress is lightened. Or she may develop addiction to a behavior that requires less money.

Brent was admitted to our Alpha Teen Unit when he was thirteen. Because of their own difficulties, his parents had often left him with grandparents and aunts and uncles or anyone who would take him in. He came to us with a deep feeling of abandonment. He desperately wanted someone to love him. He wanted to be part of a normal family. At his young age he had already had several sexual relationships with older women (most of them were in their late teens). He was hoping to get them pregnant so they would need him and not send him away.

Brent clung to each girl, trying to draw strength for his survival from her. Since the relationship came from a totally unhealthy base, they would fight and argue. In due time they would break up, and Brent would feel abandoned again. He was continually setting himself up for more abandonment, which made him look harder for someone to love him. Brent was living with his mother at the time we became involved in his life. If she was late coming home or forgot to pick him up, his feelings of abandonment were magnified. If he didn't happen to be in a relationship at the time, he would turn to drugs to dull the pain. At thirteen he was addicted to both sex and drugs.

Brent is an example of the vicious cycle that addictions can create in a person's life. As Brent learned to cope with his pain through his addictions, they become such a part of his life that without them he could not function normally. He was trying to change, but his behaviors sent him deeper and deeper into feelings of rejection and abandonment.

In the Alpha Teen Unit, Brent was in an environment that made it impossible for him to reach for his old standbys. Without sex or drugs to alter his mood, he became depressed, irritable, and hostile. His antisocial behavior would have chased away anyone in the real world who tried to help him. Fortunately, our professionals in the teen unit know how to deal with problems like Brent's. They really care for the teens and want to give them a new start on life.

It is very possible for someone like Brent to jump from one addiction to another. The problem is not cured just because the addictive agent the person has chosen becomes unavailable. He just shifts to another agent, either psychological or chemical. If Brent couldn't find another girl to love him, he masked the pain with drugs. The shopaholic who has her credit cards revoked may turn to eating or sports or exercise.

The point is this: *The behavior is not the problem.* Behavior is only the symptom of an underlying pain. The problem is whatever lies beneath the pain—the rejection that needs to be covered up, the memories that need to be forgotten, etc. Addiction is a process, a vicious cycle.

Chapter 6

What About Healing?

We have seen that the addictive process is a cycle. Fortunately, *it is possible for the last phase in that cycle to be a complete recovery.* Complete recovery means not only discontinuing the activity, but release from the emotional control that it has on your life. For example, if you have an eating disorder, you may develop enough willpower to stop eating impulsively, but if every time you smell food your feelings are saying Eat and your will is saying No, you haven't recovered. You are just controlling your addiction. The good news is that you don't have to live with this constant battle.

An addictive behavior takes up a large portion of a person's physical and mental activity. If he simply tries to exercise self-control and remove the behavior from his life, he will be left with a large hole that the addiction previously filled. That hole must be healed, or he will soon fill it with another addiction.

I have a friend who used to be an alcoholic. For many years he lived the big-party lifestyle. Then he became a Christian and quit drinking "cold turkey." While he no longer drank, he was still addicted. If he has even one glass of wine with dinner, he will be right back into his old patterns. Furthermore, the addiction has surfaced in other areas of his life. The hole that was filled with drinking is now filled with another addiction. I can tell just by listening to his answering-machine message whether he is having a good day or a bad day. When things are going his way, he is jolly and happy. If not, he is miserable.

All of us face daily ups and downs, but my friend is completely controlled by circumstances. Life is either great, or it's awful, depending on how his life is going at the moment.

Research has shown that 60 to 80 percent of all people who suffer from addictive behaviors and try to abstain from their activity or substance of choice are back into another addictive behavior within six months. For real recovery to take place, the hole must be healed, not just filled with something else.

Bob had all the makings of an addiction. His parents were divorced, he had been sexually abused as a child, and he had a low self-esteem. He met Laurie at a skating rink. Laurie came with her own set of problems. Her mother was a polio victim, and her father frequently abused both his wife and the children. When Laurie turned sixteen her father kicked her out of the house and told her he never wanted to see her again. Without knowing each other's backgrounds, Bob and Laurie were immediately drawn to each other. As usually happens when two needy people get together, the relationship rapidly became sexual. In this case Laurie got pregnant and they got married.

Like many young people with unresolved issues from their past, Bob and Laurie drank frequently, though they would never admit to being alcoholics. Seven years into their marriage they became Christians. They immediately gave up their drinking and their drinking friends, thus proving to themselves that they were not alcoholics. But neither of them had ever dealt with their past or their need for escape, and once they quit drinking, the unmet needs that were feeding their addictions surfaced in other areas. Bob became addicted to work and church. Laurie was controlled by anger and became a rage-aholic.

When a true healing takes place, the addictive behaviors aren't just suppressed or replaced by others. The desire for the addictive substance or activity is gone, and even the need for addiction is gone. For this to happen, we must look at where the need for escape comes from, and we must deal with the real cause of the problem and not just the symptom. The addiction is a symptom of something that is out of balance in life.

An addiction is much like a weed growing in a garden. The garden starts out fresh and clean. The dirt is rich and ready for planting. Beautiful flowers are planted there, and the garden looks like a showpiece. Then trouble comes, and weed seeds blow in from a neighboring field and drop into the fertile soil. The seeds send down roots, and before long they have grown tall and strong. Soon the weeds start choking out the beautiful flowers that had been doing so well, and in due time they take control of the entire garden.

The gardener comes along, sees the ugly intruders, and tries to pull them out, but they are deeply rooted and refuse to budge. He wants to clean up the garden, so he gathers all his strength and pulls very hard. Each weed snaps, and the top of the weed—the obvious part—comes off. Now the garden looks clean, and the gardener is happy.

But the roots are still firmly planted, and before long, the weeds spring up again. Soon they have taken over the entire garden again. The only permanent solution is to get out the shovel, dig down deep under each weed, and remove its entire root system.

Each one of us started out in life fresh and clean, like the garden. But at some point a seed of trauma was dropped in. Some people have many seeds that come from many fields—from sexual abuse, perhaps, or from growing up in an alcoholic home, or from a hurt or disappointment. The seed takes root and the addiction starts to grow, until before long it has taken control of our life. We can try to be strong and take control of our behavior and say that we'll never do it again, but that's just cutting off the part of the addiction that shows. The roots are still strong and healthy, and they *will* grow back. The new growth may look different. You may stop drinking only to find yourself becoming a workaholic. You may go on a diet only to find yourself struggling with a consuming anger. Being strong willed and cutting the behavior out of your life doesn't get rid of the addiction. Self-control is not the same as healing.

Healing from the addiction requires getting out the shovel and digging down deep into your life, finding the root of the problem, and removing that. Once this happens, it is possible to experience a true healing from addiction and not just an exercise of willpower. Not only will the behaviors be gone; so will the desire for the behavior or substance.

Fred Littauer thought that his subscription to *Playboy* magazine was just part of being a red-blooded American male, but when he became a Christian he knew that the subscription and the magazines had to go. He removed them from his home, but every time he passed a magazine rack at the quick-stop grocery store, he felt a strong pull toward *Playboy*, *Penthouse*, and all the others. Since he was a strong Christian and spent many hours a week in Bible study, he wouldn't allow himself to yield to temptation.

Fred and his wife Florence are frequently on the road traveling from one speaking engagement to the next. Sometimes when Fred was in a remote airport or in an area where he was sure no one would recognize him, he would give in to the temptation and flip through the pages of *Playboy*. He had been able to stop his behavior and never would have thought of himself as being addicted to pornography, but the fact that he was continually drawn to it showed that it was more than just a casual interest. When the possibility of being caught was minimal, he gave in to the temptation.

In the last few years Fred has gone through intensive therapy and uncovered some unknown pain from his childhood that he had totally buried in his mind. Although he has no conscious memory of abuse, he learned that he was the victim of a form of sexual abuse both as a young boy and in his early teen years. That was the root of his addiction to pornography and other inconsistent behaviors in his life. Through therapy and continued research, reading, and prayer, Fred processed the pain and resolved the issues from his past. At first, the changes in his life were subtle, but as time passed, more and more changes became apparent.

One of the unexpected changes surfaced when Fred was in an airport several months after his therapy had concluded. He was walking through the airport as usual. This time, however, there was no pull to the newsstands. The desire to flip through the pages of *Playboy* was completely gone.

Before he dealt with the pain of his past, the abuse unknowingly ruled his life and brought about an addiction to pornography. Through self-discipline he managed to keep from giving in to the temptation, but it was always there. But when he dug up the roots of his addiction and dealt with them, he was truly healed, and even the temptation was gone.

I was recently a guest on a radio program with Dr. Patrick Carnes from the Golden Valley Institute of Behavioral Medicine in Minneapolis. As we discussed addictions, and especially addictions of a sexual nature, he told me about a major research project that his institution had just completed. Their research showed a definite connection between the type of abuse people suffer in earlier life and the type of addictions they will develop later. In fact, he says that it is possible to predict the kind of addictions a person will most likely have and how many he will have from the nature and length of the abuse he experienced as a child. While this research is new and has not been published so far as I know, it does substantiate my personal observations from working with addicted people. I have found that there is a definite connection between the abuse and the addiction. In Fred Littauer's case the abuse was sexual and so was the addiction.

The exercises in the next chapter will give you a chance to reflect on your own life and your potential for developing an addiction. If you are already addicted and you know it, the exercises may help to identify the root cause of your problem.

Many groups specialize in helping people with specific addictions. One of these, Alcoholics Anonymous, talks about "cross addictions"—the situation we've been discussing in which a person has one addiction (in this case drinking), but his behavior gets out of control in another area. AA refers to such people as "dry drunks." When a person is encouraged to stop his addictive behavior without getting to its root cause, there is little hope for real healing. Many people teach that the best you can hope for is to control the addiction. But as Christians we know that true recovery is possible.

There are three main ingredients to experiencing complete healing. We have already learned that the first step is to identify the root cause of the addiction. This is possible through God's power in our lives and the work of the Holy Spirit. Next, we need to face the problems in our past and make the changes needed in our lives. Last, we need time. Recovery doesn't happen overnight. Just as the addictive behavior took control of our lives over a period of time, so digging up the roots, throwing them away, and replacing them with healthy behavior patterns takes time.

The time needed for recovery will be different for each person. While every case is unique, I can make some generalizations based on my experience with the many cases that have come through the doors of the Alpha Counseling Center in the last seventeen years.

Some people are healed instantly. Through faith and prayer they are able to claim Psalm 30:2 as their verse: "O Lord my God, I cried to thee for help, and thou hast healed me" (RSV). But I have seen more people healed through a process. I believe that God still does the healing, but by bringing a person *through* the pain rather than just releasing him *from* it. People who experience healing over time are much better able to minister to others. Second Corinthians 1:2-4 tells us that the God of all comfort "comforts us in all our affliction, so that we may be able to comfort those who are in any affliction, with the comfort with which we ourselves are comforted by God" (RSV). After we go through the pain, God uses our experience to enrich our own lives and the lives of those around us.

The type of abuse is an important factor to consider. Usually, emotional abuse is the least detrimental and therefore requires the shortest time for recovery. Hershel, whose story I told in chapter 3, was abused by his father, who never gave him the approval and acceptance he needed as a child. He wasn't beaten, and he wasn't sexually abused. He was a victim of emotional abuse. This type of abuse is often the most difficult for the victim to recognize as abuse. Recognizing that your parents abused you is fairly easy if they beat you or molested you sexually. It's much harder to accept the fact that you were abused when you know (or believe) that your parents did their best but for some reason were unable to give you the emotional support you needed. But emotional mistreatment is abuse, and once the victim accepts this, recovery is usually not as difficult.

Sexual and physical abuse are more extreme forms of abuse and in most cases require more time for healing. People who think their parents' behavior was normal may need even more time to heal. Abuse must be accepted as abuse before the problems it has caused can be dealt with.

Other factors that affect the healing process are the frequency of the abuse, how old the victim was when it happened, whether the perpetrator was a family member or an outsider, and whether the problem was just the circumstances of life. When the abuse is part of a lifelong pattern, its effects will be more deeply embedded in the victim's life, and it will take longer to dig the problem up and treat it. When the abuse was a one-time occurrence, its symptoms may still surface through addictive behaviors, but their effect will be less, and the healing process will take less time.

Early identification of the addiction is another factor influencing the ease or difficulty of recovery. Addictive behaviors that are allowed to go unidentified and uncorrected become much more deeply embedded, and the healing process also takes more time.

Another factor affecting recovery is the age of the victim when the abuse occurred. Abuse that is perpetrated on a child who has no form of defense and no experience in life to compare it with will be more firmly rooted than something that took place in the teen or adult years. Someone who is a victim of date rape at age twenty-three will require less time for recovery than a person who was sexually abused when she was three. A twenty-three-year-old already has a sense of who she is; she has already established a basically good relationship to the world, and thus the abuse is less devastating.

Last, who was the perpetrator? If it was an immediate family member, the pain will be much deeper. In contrast, if it was someone who was personally removed from the victim, the recovery will usually be faster.

The easiest of all to treat are those abuses that are a result of circumstances. Alan, in chapter 5, who had the Corvette, was among the more fortunate ones. His life as a child was fairly normal. The problems that caused his addiction were the death of his father, a divorce, and a series of disappointing jobs. The abuse was only emotional and circumstantial, and while it played an important role in shaping his life, it did not go as deep as physical or sexual abuse in childhood would have. His problems started in his teen years and continued into adulthood, but he got ahold of his life and was able to make the necessary changes fairly early. His problem was circumstances rather than a specific person whom he had trusted to protect him. Alan was able to turn his life around quite easily. His pains had not yet surfaced into a full addiction.

What about you? Do you have addictive behaviors in your life? Do you have pains that are unprocessed? Let's take a look.

Chapter 7

How Do You Know If You Need Help?

You now understand the many aspects of addiction. You have learned that we are not just talking about the addictive behaviors themselves, such as drugs, drinking, and smoking. Perhaps for the first time in your life you realize that it is possible for a person to be addicted to things that are good in themselves. You have also learned that addiction does not happen all at once. It "grows on you." It is a process.

You may very well be asking yourself about now, "Am I addicted to anything? Do I need help?"

Fortunately, you have also discovered that you do not need to be afraid. There is hope. If you are addicted, you can receive a complete recovery. You are not stuck in a hopeless downward spiral.

You may be wondering:

- Is my love for chocolate an addiction or just good taste?
- Do I enjoy the praise and worship music at church because it gives me an opportunity to praise my Lord and Saviour, or am I using it as an escape from hidden pain?
- Does the fact that I talk to a particular friend several times a day mean that we are close friends, or am I addicted to that relationship?
- Is the healthy sex life that I thought my spouse and I had in our marriage the result of a good relationship, or am I addicted to sex?

Don't go on a wild goose chase and assume that since you like to eat you have a food addiction, or because you like your job you are a workaholic. A thing or an activity becomes an addiction (1) if it alters your mood, (2) if it provides a distraction from emotional pain, (3) if you cannot stop it when you try, and (4) if it takes up increasing amounts of your physical and mental energy. These four factors work together to create an addiction.

Do you have a problem with an addiction? The following quick quiz will help you identify addictive patterns that may exist in your life. Take a few minutes to respond with a Yes or No to the following statements:

1. I have been accused by others of doing things to excess.
2. I tend to be involved more with my own feelings or problems than with someone else's.
3. I seem to have a low tolerance for pain.
4. People often say that I am impatient.
5. I spend a lot of time thinking about a particular substance, activity, or person.
6. The amount of time or energy that I devote to this substance, activity, or person has increased over the last several years.
7. I have one or more "sacred cows" in my life such as stubbornness or a closed mind on certain issues.
8. There is an activity, substance, or person in my life that I know is not good for me or that others have said is not good for me.
9. There are particular activities that I am unable to stop once started.
10. One (or both) of my parents was an alcoholic.
11. I have difficulty turning down a sale item.
12. I was raised in a dysfunctional or broken home.
13. I become angry and irritable when I am denied access to a particular activity or substance, or contact with a particular person.
14. I indulge in a particular substance or activity that has interfered with my work, family, or social life.
15. I have a lot of pain in my life that I have not dealt with.

If you answered Yes to seven or more of these questions, you may have an addiction. Because addictions are always progressive, this exercise can help you to start dealing constructively with your addictive behaviors before they get out of control. It is critical that you address any addiction at the earliest possible stage. Early detection makes the problem much easier to deal with.

The following chart shows the typical cycle of addictive behavior. The cycle is basically the same regardless of the exact addiction.

How Addiction to an Activity Develops

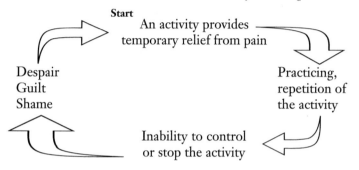

Addiction begins with an activity that provides temporary relief from pain. You take a drink, go shopping, or work out. The addictive behavior starts innocently enough, but you do it again and again because it relieves your pain and stress. In the next stage the behavior is out of control. You are unable to stop. This results in despair, guilt, and shame, which cause more pain. To deal with the pain, you again engage in the addictive behavior, and the cycle starts all over again.

The apostle Paul was aware of this dilemma when he wrote to the Roman church, "Do not let sin reign in your mortal body so that you obey its evil desires" (Romans 6:12, NIV). And in Romans 7:18 he said, "I know that nothing good lives in me, that is, in my sinful nature. For I have the desire to do what is good, but I cannot carry it out. For what I do is not the good I want to do; no, the evil I do not want to do—this I keep on doing. Now if I do what I do not want to do, it is no longer I who do it, but it is sin living in me that does it" (NIV).

Many of us are like that. The sin living in us is controlling our behaviors. People often say, "The devil made me do it." While this is a cop-out, in a sense, it is also true. The addiction in us is in control, and we behave in ways we can't stop.

As we know from the story of Achan in Joshua 7, if there is sin in the camp, it must be found, dug up, and dealt with. If an addictive behavior is controlling your life, making you do things you do not want to do, it must be identified. The following addiction assessment will help you take a closer look at your own areas of addictive behaviors. Take some time to seriously go over the following questions. They are important in helping you uncover the exact areas of addiction in your life.

Addiction Assessment

1. What are the three most important things you want to accomplish in life? Be honest with yourself. Don't list what you think you should or what your mother would have wanted, but what you really feel is most important to you.

   _____

   _____

   _____

2. Does your happiness depend on forces outside of yourself? If so, who or what makes you happy?

   _____

   _____

   _____

3. Review your checkbook register. List the three main areas of expenditure other than basic living expenses.

   _____

   _____

   _____

4. Rate your feelings of self-worth during the following ages in your life:

1-5 Poor___	Fair___	Good___	Excellent___
5-12 Poor___	Fair___	Good___	Excellent___
12-18 Poor___	Fair___	Good___	Excellent___
18-25 Poor___	Fair___	Good___	Excellent___
25 + Poor___	Fair___	Good___	Excellent___

5. What was the most traumatic event in your life?

_____

During this time, what did you do to relieve the pressure that you felt?

_____

_____

_____

6. During a normal week, what activities occupy most of your waking hours?

_____

_____

_____

7. Is there a person in your life whose sudden and permanent absence would leave you feeling tense and panicked? Who?

_____

_____

_____

Once you have completed this addiction assessment you need to consider what your answers mean. There are always reasons why we do what we do. If all three items you listed on number 1 are diverse, such as providing for your family, continuing to develop your relationship with God, and recognition in your work or area of expertise, you probably don't have a problem with addictions. However, if all three are in a similar area, such as making a lot of money, accumulating possessions, and professional recognition, this indicates that you may have an addictive behavior in the area of work. Similarly, if your three items are to look your best, accumulate possessions, and have wealth, this would indicate that your addictive behavior is in the area of shopping. Look closely at your three items. What do they say about your priorities?

If your happiness depends on anything other than yourself and your relationship with God, you should have cause for alarm. In fact, if your happiness depends solely on your relationship with God, this could be an indication that your addictive behavior is in the area of religion.

Another way to spot an addiction is to review your expenditures. Many Americans pay for most of their purchases by check or credit card, which makes it easy to identify expenses that may be excessive. If you find that a sizable amount of your income is ending up at the mall, this could be an indication of a shopping addiction. If your checkbook reveals regular checks to the local country club in amounts that are disproportionate to your other expenditures, your sports habits may have become an addiction.

A look at your self-esteem can help you to spot when and where some of your addictive behaviors got started. If you had a poor self-image as far back as you can remember, even before entering school, this could be evidence of sexual abuse or some other strong dysfunction in your childhood home. If you entered school at age five feeling pretty good about yourself but by the time you left elementary school your self-esteem dropped to poor, you will want to take a closer look at what took place in your life during those years. Perhaps your parents got a divorce or you were molested by a teacher. Wherever your self-esteem takes a dive, analyze what happened in your life at that time that might have caused the change and is probably contributing to your addictive behaviors today.

There may well be a connection between the trauma, your self-esteem, and your addiction. The way you learned to handle that trauma will have set a pattern for handling all future hurts and disappointments. The healthy way to handle it would have been to talk it through with a friend or family member at the time it happened and allow yourself to feel the hurt, anger, and related emotions. If you dealt with the pain by burying it, eating, engaging in sexual activity, or drinking, this behavior has set you up for an addiction.

If you find that your time is consumed in one major direction other than work, this would also be an indication of an addiction. If you spend sixty hours or more at work week after week, you need to look at your job as an addiction. Wall Street trader Dennis Levine was regularly putting in a sixty- to eighty-hour work week, which he said had a "numbing effect." You need to work to provide food and clothing for your family, but if your work is way out of balance to the rest of your activities—if it encompasses all of your time and attention—it may have become an addiction. Your activities need to include a variety of events, including work, leisure, and family time.

A friend of mine, Dr. Wayne Colewell, used to tell me there are only two realities in life. One is money and the other is time. These two realities tell a lot about each one of us. If we look at how we deal with these two items, we will learn a lot about ourselves and our priorities. In our society there is always time for the things that are important enough. When a friend dies, we take time out of our schedule to go to the funeral. We rearrange our life to fit it in because there will be no replay, no second chance. We make time for the things that are important to us. How we choose to spend our time tells a lot about us.

The same is true of money. We spend our money for the things that are most important to us, and the way we spend our money tells a lot about the kind of persons we are.

Since many people who struggle with addictive behaviors have more than one addiction or bounce back and forth between addictions, it is important to identify which areas in your life are addictions or have addictive tendencies. You may have found your own addictive behaviors in one of the previous sections. Keep in mind that if you have addictive behaviors, you may also have an addictive relationship—an addiction to a person. If you indicated that you would feel tense or in a panic if a particular person was suddenly out of your life, you may have an addiction to that person. It is normal to feel a sense of uptightness if that person is your spouse. In marriage our lives become so intertwined that losing our mate has been proven to be one of the most difficult adjustments. No matter whose stress charts you are looking at, you will always find "Death of a spouse" to be one of the top stressors in life.

The key issue in an addiction to a person is the panic that takes place at the thought of losing that person. This is more difficult when it comes to a spouse because of the strong emotional ties that exist even in a normal relationship. However, many people do become addicted to their spouses, and if you think this might have happened to you, you need to determine for sure. It is possible to know. Ask yourself, Am I overly dependent on my husband or wife? Do I get most of my emotional support from him or her?

Addiction to people can take place in a number of ways. It is easy for the parishioner in a church to become addicted to the pastor. The pastor illuminates his life with spiritual understanding. He is usually an authority figure, as well as someone who is loving and kind. Every week the pastor imparts words of life from God's Word. He's very visible to all the people and highly regarded. Therefore, for you to spend individual time with him may feel very fulfilling. An unmet need for acceptance by your father could propel you toward an addiction to your pastor. I have used the example of a pastor, but it could be any father figure—an older person who is an authority figure. Examples might be an employer or even your therapist. These relationships can grow to the point of an unhealthy dependency.

Write down any thoughts or emotions that have been stirred up as you have examined the addictive processes in your life. Identifying that there is a problem in your life and seeing where it comes from is a major step on your road to recovery.

PART II
RECOVERY

Chapter 8

Do You Have a Problem?

Since the addictive behavior is really only the symptom of a problem that has taken root, we must examine our addiction and find out where its roots come from.

Jean was addicted to motherhood. Motherhood is a good thing, but when it takes on the characteristics of an addiction, it becomes a smothering relationship for both the parent and the child.

A natural, healthy mother's role is to develop children who are mature and who will learn to get along without her. With that aim, a mother will not be devastated when her children grow up and move away to begin their own lives. An emotionally healthy mother has her own interests in addition to her parenting role.

However, Jean had thrown herself into being a mother. If you met her on a street corner, you would immediately hear about the recent awards her children had won and the great grades they were getting in school, and you would be admiring their smiling little faces. She always put her children's needs before her own, and her home was the neighborhood gathering place. If one of her children was on a team, she became the coach. If they were in a play, she helped design the sets. She taught their Sunday-school classes, and her children were seldom without her. Everyone could see that she was truly a "good" mother. She was such a good mother, in fact, that every other mother in her circle of acquaintances felt inferior in comparison.

Jean got great satisfaction out of being known as "Mom" to every child she came in contact with. Her identity was totally wrapped up in her role, and she seemed to enjoy proving herself a better mother than anyone else. To her, being a good mother meant that she was a good person.

Let's examine this as an addictive behavior in light of what we have discussed about addictions.

An addiction has to be mood altering. Jean grew up in what appeared to be a loving atmosphere. She had good, church-going, godly parents. She was the first of five children. However, Jean's mother never gave her any compliments, so she never felt that she was good at anything. Yet her mother expected her to care for all her younger brothers and sisters.

Jean's feelings of low self-worth were verified when she participated in a championship spelling bee. She beat all the fourth-graders in their county, but her mother didn't attend because the spelling bee was on Wednesday night, and she couldn't miss prayer meeting. The boost that winning the spelling bee could have given to Jean's sense of self-worth was diminished, and in fact demolished, by the fact that her mother did not care enough about her to show up.

Part of Jean's motivation for motherhood was to be sure that her children never had to face the hurt and humiliation she felt. *She will be there for her kids!*

In some cases a single incident, such as the day Jean's mother chose to attend her prayer meeting instead of Jean's spelling bee, can set the stage for future addiction. Certainly, repeated behavior such as that is a setup for addiction. This was the cause of Jean's low self-image, which was one of the things that set her up for an addiction. She altered the bad mood of her low self-image by creating another mood— mothering. Assuring herself that she was the best mother possible, to the point of being a better mother than anyone else, made her feel good about herself.

An addiction has to provide a distraction from the emotions or feelings of pain. In addition to Jean's childhood pain, she lost an infant daughter. She still had three boys, though, and by pouring her life into those boys she was able to dull the pain of losing her daughter. Motherhood provided a distraction for her.

An addiction must be progressive. Jean didn't start out to be supermom. She just helped out in her children's classroom. But the teacher's praise for her efforts felt good—it altered her mood. Soon she had progressed from being an occasional classroom helper to being there for every event.

An addiction occupies a disproportionate amount of time. Jean became like her mother. Her mother's addiction was to church or religion. She couldn't even miss church for an important family event. Her life was out of balance. Jean's life was also out of balance. She never developed any significant interests outside of mothering. Being a mother occupied all her time. She did go back to school to get a degree in teaching. After all, that made her a better mother.

One by one, Jean's children grew up and left home to start their own lives. When she had just one child left, she worked at his school, drove him to school each day, spent the day with him, and drove him home at night. But when he graduated from high school and went away to college, Jean had no more reason for living. Now all her children were grown and out of the house. She suddenly had an empty nest, and, like so many women before her, she discovered she had been a mother to the exclusion of all else.

Let's look at your addictions. What did the Addiction Assessment show you about your values and priorities?

Some of the areas that occupy a lot of your time and energy may be healthy. Others may have become an addiction. Maybe you discovered that work is an overwhelming focus in your life. Is it really an addiction, or is it just something that is out of balance? To find out, ask yourself, Does it alter my mood? If you find yourself spending more time at work when you are angry or facing a difficulty in your life, then your job has become a release for your stress. Yes, it would alter your mood.

Now go on to the next aspect of an addiction. Does it provide a distraction from emotions or feelings of pain? By keeping yourself overworked you have no time for looking at yourself. Work can very easily be a distraction.

Next you ask yourself, Has it progressed? You may have started staying at the office late during a crisis time in your life. When you discovered that it dulled the pain, you began staying late almost every night. To be an addiction, an activity must progress from an innocent behavior to a consuming passion.

Last, you need to evaluate *whether this activity occupies a disproportionate amount of your time.* As I mentioned earlier, if you regularly spend over sixty hours a week at work, you should consider that "disproportionate." An exception would be if your financial status is in such poor shape that you are struggling to work two jobs just to keep food on the table.

A behavior needs to have all four aspects of an addiction to be an addiction. Before you look at your own behaviors, let's run another behavior through the addiction definition.

Suppose that shopping is very important to you. You need to ask yourself, Does shopping alter my mood? For many of us, going shopping is a good change of pace, and it provides a release from the daily pressures of life. So you can say, Yes, shopping alters my mood. However, that alone is not enough to declare it an addiction.

You also need to ask whether shopping provides a distraction from your feelings of pain. If you find that every time you feel stressed you want to go shopping, then shopping does provide a distraction from the real cause of that stress. I remember an old friend of my mother's, Elsa. She used to get extreme headaches on a regular basis. She went to doctor after doctor, but no one could find a cause or a cure. Then one day she went to a psychologist, who had her keep a list of the times when she had a headache. She discovered that she got a headache whenever she was unable to go shopping. This was back when all the stores were closed on Sundays. Every Sunday, Elsa would get physically sick at the thought of not being able to go shopping. Shopping was her addiction.

The third thing to ask yourself is whether the behavior or activity is progressive. If your activity started out simple and small, and now you are doing it much more frequently, then it surely has progressed.

Last, ask yourself, Does this activity occupy a disproportionate amount of my time? A good way to answer that question is to determine whether your behavior is frequently in the way of other things you should or would like to do. To stay with our shopping example, you find yourself with a half-hour of free time, so you go shopping. While at the store you get so involved that you completely lose track of time and are late for your next obligation. Maybe you are late to pick up the kids or miss getting to the bank because of your addiction to shopping.

Once you have evaluated all the important areas in your life in light of the factors that cause addictive behaviors, you should have a fairly good idea of the problems in your life. So now you know what your problems are, which is one of the biggest parts of the battle. But you didn't just decide to drink too much or be too active. Those problems came from somewhere—from some pain in your life—and you need to find out the source of that pain.

Jean's addiction to motherhood was caused by two factors. First were the issues from her childhood. Her mother never gave her the approval she needed. Jean felt that church was more important to her mother than she was. This set her up to need something to give her a feeling of value, something to help her feel good. However, there was a second factor in Jean's life, which set off this feeling of low self-worth and started her addiction rolling. Just as she was entering into motherhood, with a need for approval and value, one of her children died, and this brought the addictive behavior into the area of mother-hood. If the crisis in her life had been financial, her need for approval might have been fulfilled through getting a job, and she might well have developed an addiction to work, commonly called workaholism.

Let's look at Hershel, the workaholic from chapter 3. His basic need was similar to Jean's. His father failed to give him the approval he needed to develop into a strong, healthy adult. Instead, his father said, "Why can't you be more like your brother?" Looking deeper into the family structure, we find that Hershel's brother was a successful executive in a large corporation. Hershel's basic need was approval from his father, and his father's comment that he should be more like his brother pushed him in the direction of a work addiction.

Now let's look at your addictive behaviors. Where did they come from? Since addictions are often directly related to the pain that lies at their source, we can begin our search for the pain by looking at the addictive behavior itself. If your addictions are sexual, the pain may stem from sexual abuse. If your addictions lie in the area of shopping, exercise, or perfectionism, you may have felt unattractive as a child, or your parents may have compared you to others, saying they were better or prettier. If your addiction is to studying or school, your father or mother may have told you that you were unintelligent and unworthy. Many people get degree on top of degree in an effort to prove to themselves and their parents that they are not stupid.

Irene attended a seminar I was giving. She had several master's degrees and was working on another one. When I asked what she did that required so many degrees, she said that she didn't do anything with them. She didn't even work. She just liked to study. However, with a bit of probing I discovered that her family was a mess. Her children didn't speak to her, and her husband lived at the other end of the house.

So I asked her, "When you were a child, did anyone tell you that you were stupid?"

"Oh, yes!" she said. "My father always told me that my sister was the pretty one and I was the stupid one."

"And what's the first thing you do when you get another degree?" I asked.

"I call up my father and tell him what I've done."

"And what does he say?"

"His simple response is, 'That's nice.'"

Because Irene doesn't get her father's approval, she signs up for another class. Her addiction is directly related to the pain of her past.

Many addictions are not so clearly connected to the exact source of the pain. A person who is addicted to drugs isn't addicted because his mother gave him too many aspirins when he was a child. Walt, whose problem is TV sports, isn't addicted because his father was a football player. In these cases the addiction and the pain that causes it are not directly related. Your addictions may be like these, which will make finding the exact source of your pain more difficult.

Let's look at Walt and his addiction to TV sports. The opportunity to jump up and down gave him a way to vent his anger in an acceptable way. The key here is the anger. But where did the anger come from? Walt grew up in a dysfunctional home where expressing feelings was not allowed. Furthermore, he didn't feel that his parents accepted him.

You can begin identifying the source of your pain by asking yourself what you receive from your addictive behavior. What's the "payoff"? Don't be surprised if at first you don't think the addiction is giving you any benefit. Remember that all behavior is purposeful. Write down how you feel before your addictive behavior, while you are involved in it, and afterward.

Walt thought the TV sports were simply an avenue for friendship, but on closer examination he realized that he felt a great sense of relief after each game. His "payoff" was a release from anger, which helped him to enjoy life more.

Some people have no memories of childhood pain, and they think it is impossible to trace its origin. The addiction is there, but they have no idea why. It is like the bear in the woods story. You go out camping, and you see bear tracks all around your tent. It's easy to tell a bear was there, but there's no bear. What we do see is the results of the bear. So even if you have no memory of a painful event, you have the bear tracks—the addiction that indicates something happened.

If you have the bear tracks but no memories, then you may need outside help. You might want to seek the help of a professional who specializes in memory retrieval. However, I believe that the Christian has another source of outside help: prayer. Ask the Lord to reveal to you these "secret things" that you can't remember. Pray that He will bring to your mind the events which took place in your life that you need to know. Luke 12:2, 3 promises that "nothing is covered up that will not be revealed, or hidden that will not be made known. Therefore whatever you have said in the dark shall be heard in the light, and what you have whispered in private rooms shall be proclaimed upon the housetops" (RSV). I have seen God do miraculous things in answering the prayers of those who come to Him earnestly seeking the truth. And the resulting truth "sets them free" (see John 8:32).

Chapter 9

Do You Need Professional Help?

Hershel was a successful businessman. His company had grown into an empire, and he had the respect of everyone in his industry. He had reached the goals he set for himself. His wife Lee had the right kind of car, and his kids went to the right private schools. You may remember him from chapter 3.

Hershel was a model workaholic of the 1980s. Each achievement needed to be topped by something bigger and better. His wife, Lee, had long ago lost interest in having another diamond or a bigger house. For several years she had been nagging Hershel to come home earlier, to be there for the family events, and to invest in their children's lives. One night they had a fight, and Hershel promised to do better. And he did. The next time his son played in Little League, Hershel was there. He missed the first two innings, but at least he was there. Unfortunately, that's as far as his commitment ever got. Always, the first event after an argument with Lee caused him to pull himself away from work in order to please his wife and family. But the next night he worked late, and the following event he missed altogether.

Lee found this pattern of behavior repeating itself over and over again. It got to the point where she created a fight just to get Hershel to attend an event she felt was really important.

Hershel felt that Lee was being unreasonable. Wasn't he keeping her in stylish clothes; a good car; and a modern, comfortable home? She ought to be happy! She didn't have to work, which meant *she* could be there for the kids' various little events. His father was never at any of his childhood events, and that didn't seem to have caused any problems in his life. Their kids would be OK too.

Hershel really did love Lee and the kids and didn't want to make them unhappy. So whenever Lee made a scene over his absence, he tried to appease her. He'd announce to his secretary and his managers that he was no longer available to them after 4:00 p.m. Sure enough, he'd leave work by 4:30 for a day or two. Then his resolve seemed to fade, and business problems came up that only he could handle. How could he leave?

This cycle went on and on. Hershel would fix the situation himself, with brief success, and then fail again, with a resolve to try harder next time.

Let me ask you, Did Hershel need help?

Yes, Hershel needed help. Why? Because he didn't see his problem as an addiction. Most of us who have an addiction don't recognize the problem for what it is. The word *addiction* sounds so strong. It brings up images of a drug addict making a deal in a dark alley or of a bum sleeping on the sidewalk of a big city with a brown-bagged bottle clutched in his hand. We think, "Certainly I'm not addicted. I'm a good family person, with honest intentions. I'm a Christian, not an addict!" But many Christians *do* have addictive behaviors.

Once we see our problem as it really is and accept that it has reached the point of addiction, we need to accept that we need help.

When Hershel came to us at Alpha Counseling Center, he wasn't there for help. He was there to make his wife happy and keep the family intact. However, after a few visits he saw that he was addicted to his work and that he needed help. He realized that he had tried unsuccessfully many times on his own. We discussed the characteristics of an addiction with him, and he began to see the severity of his situation. He could see that work offered him a sense of accomplishment and worth that he had longed for since his childhood. Work altered his mood. It also provided a distraction from his feelings of pain. Hershel realized that his overwork was getting worse. It was progressive. And it certainly occupied a disproportionate amount of his time. With this realization, Hershel accepted the fact that he had a problem, that he was addicted to his work. That was the first step.

My hope for you is that by now you have discovered whether addiction is a problem in your life. Hershel had to be forced into counseling to get to that point. Through the understanding and examination you have been through in the previous chapters, you should be able to save yourself both the time and expense of this stage of counseling. But you may still need help. Once a situation has reached the point of addiction, additional help is usually necessary.

However, help doesn't have to mean going into long-term therapy. It might mean that some counseling with a specialist trained in your area of need will be necessary, but help is available in ways other than just therapy. We have divided the remaining sections of this book into the various ways of getting help.

Getting help involves getting support, learning all you can about your particular addiction, getting objective feedback on your progress, and allowing time for healing. All of these things are available to you through a good counseling program. But for those who can't find a good program, can't afford counseling, or have difficulty with the entire concept of therapy, much of the help that is needed can be found through other sources. A counseling center offers the convenience of all the resources in one setting, and those with the finances, either personally or through insurance, may find that a Christian counseling center is the best choice.

Getting help is not a sign of weakness; rather, it is a sign of honesty and strength. When we acknowledge that we cannot fix our problems on our own, we allow God to work in our lives. Second Corinthians 12:9, 10 tells us that it is in our weaknesses that He is made strong. It is only through God's power that true healing can be found.

I have seen God work in many different ways in people's lives. I have a friend who was in the hospital for back surgery. The night before her surgery the doctor took some additional X-rays just to be sure he knew exactly where the problem was. But when he got the results, the back problem was gone—healed! She went home, and the surgery was never performed. Why does God heal a few people with a miraculous, instantaneous healing, while the rest of us need treatment by a specialist?

Emotional or psychological problems are much the same as physical problems. The difference is that when we have a physical problem we wouldn't hesitate to go to the doctor. We know we can't operate on ourselves, and reaching out for help isn't considered a sign of weakness. God may choose to heal the pain of your past instantly, but

I have seen far more cases in which the healing came through the loving help of someone who could provide the compassion and understanding needed for the addict to face the necessary changes in his life.

Another person provides the support you need—understanding, insight into the nature of your situation, and objective feedback. This will help you keep the time frame for healing in perspective.

Recovery from addiction usually requires help—help from God, help from friends, and help from someone who's been there. It's time for you to reach out for help.

Chapter 10

What Is Your Addiction?

As life gets more complicated and economic pressures intensify, we are increasingly in need of an escape from the stresses we face. In America's recent history the outside world provided a sense of security. Our jobs were secure, and we trusted our government and our military to protect us. Nature had wrapped us in a "security blanket."

But today the human race has become an endangered species. The factors beyond our control that used to leave us feeling safe have been torn from us, leaving many of us with emotional turmoil. We feel unsure of our place in life. I believe this situation has created an increase in addictive behaviors in our country.

While this may be a frightening thought, it is also good for those who are caught in the addictive process. The increase in addictions has brought new understanding of the entire concept. We now know that addictions include more than drugs and alcohol. They include a variety of both good and bad behaviors. Addiction occurs when one or more of these behaviors becomes all-consuming and knocks our life out of balance.

As addictive behaviors have been brought into the light, much more information has become available to help us understand our own patterns. As we discussed in the previous chapter, those who take advantage of several forms of help and education usually recover much more quickly than those who only attend a support group or attend a seminar.

Reading is one way to get help. You are reading this book, and that is important because it will open your eyes to the unhealthy behaviors in your life. It has been written with the intent of showing you activities and behaviors that may be perfectly healthy in some cases but that can become an addiction that is nearly as destructive as drugs or alcohol. While shopping, hobbies, church attendance, exercise, sports, and fellowship are not inherently bad, they can become addictions and be as ruinous as the things you have always known were bad for you. They may not be chemically addictive as substance abuse is, and they may not destroy your brain, but addictions to good things can be just as detrimental to your relationships and your emotions as substance abuse is to your body.

While many more people are suffering with this type of addiction, more help is also available today than at any previous time in history. Once you have discovered what an addiction is, have accepted that you are addicted, and have gotten help, and found new friends (more about this in chapter 13), the next part of the process is to learn all you can about your particular form of addiction. I already mentioned books as an excellent place to start. Read everything you can find on the addiction that is troubling you. You will soon begin to understand how you got into your addictive state. Another excellent way to gain insight is seminars and workshops that are offered in your area. These will help to speed your recovery. The more you know about your addictive process, the easier it will be for you to find freedom from it.

We have seen many examples of people whose lives and professions have been torn apart because of their addictive behaviors. Some of those whose lives we have shared were able to correct their addictions before everything collapsed around them, while others were awakened by the shattering of their lives and homes.

Randy was one whose life crashed around him and forced him to look at his own issues. He had allowed his hobbies to overcome him. No one thought he was addicted. They just thought he was obsessed—maybe a little odd—but it never occurred to anyone, least of all to Randy himself, that collecting cars could be an addiction. For many people it is not, but for Randy it became an escape he couldn't live without.

Randy's wife Terese had packed up herself and the kids and walked out, leaving him with nothing but an empty garage and lots of free time. The hobby had started gradually, but before long, both the garage and his hours were full. He was in debt over the cars and had no other interest whatsoever in life. He worked each day, but he lived to get home and tinker with his toys. His work began to slip, and his supervisor suggested he get some counseling through a therapy program that his company offered.

Randy attended, and he began to see that cars had become an addiction. He had no friends except the guys he saw at the car-club meetings, and he saw that he needed to broaden his friendships. He needed to develop relationships with people who had other interests. The support group began to fill that need in his life, and slowly Randy grew into a vital, interesting human being again.

His counselor suggested that Randy fill some of his leisure time with reading. He recommended several books. Learning about the entire addictive process brought his own problem into the light. Seeing in black and white what had happened in his life made the pieces fit together. Understanding that he was not alone, that others suffered with loneliness and rejection just as he did, was the key that sent his healing process into its final phases.

Perhaps you, like Randy, have had your eyes opened. You realize that you have allowed one or more activities in your life to dominate your thoughts and behaviors. If you have begun to make changes in your life, reading books on the subject of addiction will help move your recovery along. So much has been written on the subject in the last few years that it would be impossible to give you a complete reading list, and more books (like this one) are being released every day. The following reading list is a good starting place. These books offer sound, biblically based information about the general subject of addiction and some of the specific types of addiction. While not all the authors agree with me or each other, reading their material will give you a continuing education on the subject and speed your healing process.

My friend Steve Arterburn has written several books dealing with addictions. Any or all of them will be helpful to you:

- *Hooked on Life: How to Totally Recover From Addictions and Dependency* by Stephen Arterburn and Tim Timmons, Oliver-Nelson Books.
- *Toxic Faith: Understanding and Overcoming Religious Addiction* by Stephen Arterburn and Jack Felton, Oliver-Nelson Books.
- *Addicted to Love: Recovering From Unhealthy Dependencies in Love,*

Romance, Relationships, and Sex by Stephen Arterburn, Servant.

Some other books that may be helpful to you are:

- *Fatal Attractions: Overcoming Our Secret Addictions* by Bill Perkins, Harvest House Publishers.
- *When Addiction Comes to Church: Helping Yourself and Others Move Into Recovery* by Melinda Fish, Chosen Books.
- *Private Obsessions: Freedom From Secret Sins and Hidden Habits* by Lee Ezell, Word Books.
- *We Are Driven and the Compulsive Behaviors America Applauds* by Drs. Robert Hemfelt, Frank Minirth, and Paul Meier, Thomas Nelson Publishers.
- *Love Hunger: Recovery From Food Addiction* by Drs. Frank Minirth, Paul Meier, Robert Hemfelt, and Sharon Sneed, Fawcett.
- *Healing Life's Hidden Addictions: Overcoming the Closet Compulsions That Waste Time and Control Your Life* by Dr. Archibald Hart, Servant.

Begin your reading program with the books that address the specific areas of your need, and then continue with those that are more general in nature. If there are no books available in your specific area, start with those that deal with the overall subject of addictive behaviors.

Chapter 11

What Set the Addiction Up?

An addiction is like a domino train. All the pieces are there, set up and ready to go. They will stand still and upright until someone pushes the first one. From there, the other dominos quickly fall, one after another.

The addictive process begins with issues in life that set you up. The pieces are all there, but you are not addicted until something knocks that first piece over. Then it is like some uncontrollable force takes over, and all the other pieces of your life fall apart. You are addicted. It is important to look back at the early signs of a problem. They will be a piece in the puzzle of your addiction.

What was the first push of your domino train?

As we saw in the previous chapter, for Randy it was Terese leaving him. Prior to the first domino falling, Randy had enjoyed cars and worked with them, but they were not an addictive behavior. When Terese left him, it set off a lot of feelings that were hidden by his comfortable situation.

When the external factors in his life were secure, the inner conflict could be held at bay. But when the stability left his life, the unresolved issues of his childhood churned inside, and the pain needed a way of escape. For Randy the collapse of his marriage is not what caused the addiction, it was what set the addiction up and brought it to the surface.

By recognizing Randy's first domino we can go back into his childhood to see what else is there and why a separation was so traumatic for him. Other people go through divorces and don't become addicted. Why did he?

Look at your life. Try to find the event or experience in your life that set up your addictive behaviors. It may be a crisis such as Randy faced, or it may be something more simple. Whatever it was, understanding what that first domino was will give you insight into the past and what made you vulnerable. Examine your addiction and see what happened to you just prior to that behavior becoming so central.

It may have been a job change or a change in marital status. For others, their new faith and the fellowship of the church may be the thing that set the addiction in process. A spirit of competition among the guys at work could open you up to an addiction such as exercise or sports.

By understanding what set the addiction up, you can more clearly look at your past and find the root cause of your problem. Addictive behaviors are a way of dealing with pain. If we have nothing from which we need relief, we are not likely to become involved in addictions, especially those we have been discussing that are not chemically based.

There is usually a connection between the event that set the addiction up and the pain from our past that the addiction protects us from. That first domino in the train is overreaction to the event that set up our addictive behavior. As we saw in Randy's case, a major crisis set up his addiction. When Terese left him, he overreacted. Many people get divorced but don't go into addictive behaviors. Any time we overreact to something in our lives, it gives us a clue to other problems that may be hidden beneath our emotional surface.

Joyce and Jonathan came to see me for marriage counseling. Jonathan had been unaware there were any problems in the marriage until one day Joyce overreacted to a simple mistake he made. They had no children and had developed a pattern of eating breakfast together before they went to work. Jonathan saw this as a time to read the paper, while Joyce wanted to discuss the day at hand. She didn't communicate her displeasure to Jonathan, though, until the day she overreacted.

Joyce had been eating her breakfast, feeling ignored, when she asked Jonathan to pass her the salt. Without pausing from his reading, Jonathan passed her the pepper. Frustration over his lack of attention had reached the boiling point in her mind, and when Jonathan passed her the pepper, it "proved" to her that he truly didn't care. She threw the pepper shaker down and smashed her plate. Then she screamed at Jonathan, grabbed the newspaper, and tore it to shreds.

Joyce overreacted to a simple mistake, but that overreaction was a result of cumulative feelings. For years she had been thinking that her husband didn't listen to her and wasn't paying any attention to her. His little error proved to her she was right.

While Joyce's behavior was an overreaction to the immediate situation, the incident showed that there was a much deeper problem in their marriage, and it got them to come for counseling, to work on their relationship.

So it is with our addictive behaviors. That first domino creates a reaction that alerts us to the need to look deeper into our lives and examine our past.

Chapter 12

Where Did Your Problem Come From?

You have started on the journey toward healing by recognizing the addiction in your life and realizing that you need help. Admitting that a problem exists is always the first step. But before you can go further you must uncover the root cause of your addiction.

You can quit drinking. You can force yourself to be out of the office every day by 4:00. You can know you have a problem, get help, change your friends, and read all you can. But unless you deal with the reason for your susceptibility to addiction in the first place, all of that will just be a Band-Aid on top of the wound. To be most effective, identifying and dealing with the root cause of an addictive behavior usually requires the help of a counselor who is trained to recognize the symptoms of past pain.

Randy thought his problem came from Terese leaving him, but that was just the problem which tipped him off that he had a deeper problem. The real problem stemmed from the rejection he had felt from his father as a child. Terese's departure brought back all the hurts he had buried from his childhood. They had lain dormant in his mind for years.

Randy hoped Terese would fill his need for love and support, and this expectation put unrealistic demands on her. Through his therapy Randy discovered where his real problem came from and was able to deal with the issues of rejection in his life. Once he discovered the root cause and dealt with it, the need for his addiction lessened. He spent his time in a variety of new ways that added balance to his life.

81

If you have clear memories of painful experiences in the past, you will want to take some time to look at them in a new way. You may have thought that these events were unrelated to your life today.

However, if you do not have conscious memories of your childhood and cannot think of anything in your past that your addictive behaviors are providing an escape from, you may need to seek counsel from someone who specializes in repressed childhood trauma.

While a good counselor with experience in uncovering memories may be needed, the following exercises, which you can do on your own, will give you insight into your past.

Exercises

Devotional time. The first thing I suggest is that you have a regular time for Bible study and prayer. Spending time with God is cleansing in itself, and while this does not usually bring back bad memories on its own, it does provide you with a strong faith as a foundation for when the memories do return. During your time of prayer, ask the Holy Spirit to reveal to you the memories you need to deal with in the healing of your addictive behaviors. There is power in prayer, and the Holy Spirit will bring back the memories you need to address. Even if you have clear memories of difficult times in your past, the Holy Spirit will reveal to you which of the events in your life need to be dealt with more completely.

Talking with relatives. If you have brothers and/or sisters, talk with them about what your childhood home was like. Discuss the various events with them. They may have a different perspective on a situation that has affected your life, which can open up new areas of understanding for you.

Conversations with your parents can often provide additional insight. To avoid making your parents feel threatened, start by asking them about family traditions and how they came to be. Ask about their relationship with one another. Ask about aunts and uncles who were a regular part of your life, what they did for a living, why they came to visit, and whether their visits were a good time or a difficult time. Ask about the houses you lived in and whether the family was happy in each one. Did any significant things take place in each house? What about teachers and school activities?

Journaling. It is important that you keep a journal of your thoughts and feelings as you pray and as you review your past through old family pictures and conversations with your brothers and sisters. Your journal can be a specially made book, a spiral-bound school notebook, a loose-leaf notebook, or even your computer. Use whatever is most comfortable for you. Record your thoughts and feelings, especially those that come to you as a reaction to your prayers, your conversations with family members, and reviewing old photos. Work on your journal every day. Over a period of time you will see patterns begin to emerge. You'll be surprised at the patterns that jump out at you as you go back through your journal and evaluate what you have written.

The questions they won't answer. Because of all that is understood today about the effect of the past on our present behavior, many parents or siblings may feel threatened when you start digging into the past. They may tell you to let well enough alone or refuse to answer your questions. That can be very useful information too. Make notes in your journal about the areas that make them feel uncomfortable. The questions they won't answer may be as helpful as those they do.

Family pictures. Gather up as many family pictures and old movies as you can find, and review them prayerfully. Any time one of them triggers a flood of emotion, ask the Holy Spirit to reveal to you what about that place or person has caused an emotional reaction. Be aware of which pictures cause a reaction in you. You may find, for example, that a picture of a certain house is consistently uncomfortable or that seeing a particular relative is difficult for you.

Dreams. As you continue looking at your past, you may find that you have dreams or even nightmares that expose new memories. Don't discount them as "just a dream." Dreams are one way that our bodies let out our pent-up emotions. Freud said, "Dreams are the royal road to the unconscious." If you have asked the Holy Spirit to reveal to you the memories that are important for you in your healing process, you may find that dreams are one of the ways He reveals them. Keep a paper and pencil by your bed. If you are awakened by a dream, jot down the essence of it before you forget it. As you do this, you may find a common thread in your dreams that will add insight to your search. Keep a record of your dreams and how you felt during the dream in your journal.

Finding the root cause of addictive behavior requires that you become both a historian and an explorer on a journey to open up the past so you can clean up the past and how you respond in the present.

Chapter 13

Are Your Friends Contributing to Your Problem?

Friends are an important part of our lives. John tells us that Jesus commanded us to love one another as He has loved us (see John 13:34), so clearly our relationships with each other are important to God. But as we begin making changes in our behavior patterns, it is important to examine our friendships and determine whether they are adding to our problems or helping us to heal. Proverbs cautions us over and over to be careful about the kinds of people we choose for friends. In chapter 18:24 Solomon reminds us that "some friends may ruin you. But a real friend will be more loyal than a brother" (The Everyday Bible, New Century Version).

Gary's friends from work started out as associates at the office, but as the relationships grew, so did their influence over him. The guys teased him about being a prude. When they headed off to happy hour, he always went home. But things at home weren't like they used to be. Now that there were children, it seemed that Lisa never had time for him anymore. Lisa worked hard too, but with the kids to care for, she found it impossible to keep up the house all by herself, and even with two incomes, money was always a problem.

One day Gary gave in and decided to join the guys. Why not? Dinner was rarely ready on time these days anyway, and he didn't think he could face vacuuming, laundry, and diapers one more time, so he went to happy hour. What a discovery. No wonder they called it happy hour! This was much more pleasant than going home. The waitresses were cute and wore really short skirts—of course the guys had a great time. Besides, after a couple of drinks the problems at home seemed much easier to face, and the traffic wasn't nearly so bad later in the evening. Even work was better. The fellows made him feel more like a part of the team. They weren't just the guys from the office anymore. Now they were his friends.

Gary became addicted, not to alcohol, but to the good times, the escape from a life that had become unpleasant. The addiction progressed to the point that Gary dreaded going home. Once he got home Lisa was mad that he'd been gone so long and she'd had to take care of all the family responsibilities alone.

What seemed like an innocent activity had grown out of hand. Eventually things got so bad between them that Lisa kicked him out. This brought a rude awakening in Gary's life. He realized that he loved Lisa and the children and didn't want to be separated from them.

Gary's addiction to the good times at happy hour had progressed so gradually that he was unaware of its power over him until he tried to straighten out his life. Now he was forced to face his shortcomings. He *had* to deal with his addictions. Gary went for therapy and was trying to deal with his situation, but every day there were "the guys." With those friends, the temptations never went away. Gary had to ask for a transfer to another branch in the company so he could start over. It meant a cut in pay, but it made all the difference in his progress.

Take a look at the people you spend significant amounts of time with, especially those whose companionship you feel good about. Do they encourage your negative behaviors, or do they add balance to your life?

We have about a dozen teenage residents at our Alpha Boys Ranch at any given time. Most of these young men have had trouble with drugs or other addictive behaviors. Bo, as he liked to be called, had been living with us for about seven months. He was sixteen years old and before coming to the ranch had been failing in school. He frequently left the high-school campus to do drugs with his friends. The counselor at school said Bo needed a new environment in order to change. Someone recommended the Alpha Boys Ranch, and Bo moved in.

During the time he was there, he responded well. He was catching up on his schoolwork and had been able to stay off drugs for several months. Bo became one of the stronger young men at our facility and an example to the others of the change that can take place in a person's life.

As the holidays approached, Bo got nervous about going home. At the ranch he had accomplished something that mattered to him. Here he was a leader. At home his friends were older. He was the kid and they were the leaders, and they led him astray. While he wanted to see his family, he was aware that his old friends still held an influence over him.

He did go home, and during that time he connected with his former friends. They encouraged him to use drugs again, and Bo gave in. His parents were anxious to get Bo back into Alpha's healthy environment, but when they hugged and tearfully waved goodbye to him at the train station, Bo had other ideas. Somewhere between his hometown and the Alpha Boys Ranch, he got off the train and never made it back to the ranch. Since his friends were older and had their own cars and apartments, they made it easy for Bo to slip back into his old patterns.

Even if your addictive behaviors don't include drugs, your friends may be just as damaging to your healing process as Bo's friends were to him.

Cindy was addicted to exercise. You may remember her from chapter 1. She became so absorbed with working out that little by little she had no time for the friends in other areas of her life. She spent all her time with the friends she met at the gym. Since they too were heavily into exercise, they saw nothing wrong with her behaviors. In fact, they fed her addiction by applauding each new athletic goal she achieved and each competition she won.

Under normal circumstances exercise is a perfectly healthy activity, but it became an addictive behavior for Cindy. When her injury suddenly pulled the rug out from under her, she was forced to face her problem, and she realized that her friends at the gym were contributing to her problem.

Our friends should support us and add balance to our lives. They should be strong in areas where we are weak and thus offer us a challenge and a role model. We may be strong in an area where that same friend is weak. Everyone grows when we build friendships with those who help us and those whom we can help. Proverbs 27:17 says, "Iron can sharpen iron. In the same way, people can help each other."

Ecclesiastes 4:9, 10 says, "Two people are better than one. They get more done by working together. If one person falls the other can help him up. It is bad for the person who is alone when he falls. No one is there to help him" (The Everyday Bible, New Century Version).

What about your friends? Do they sharpen you and lift you up? Do they come from a diverse background of interests? Or, do they like the same things you are attracted to and perhaps are addicted to?

We talked about Alan in chapter 5. While he had many of the characteristics in his life that lead to addictive behaviors, he had friends from a variety of different areas. Alan's hobby, his car, could have become an addiction for him, but because he continued to have interests other than the members of his car club, he was able to change his course by making a change in his life. Alan went back to school to get his master's degree in counseling. Rather than shrinking his sphere of influence, he expanded it and made many new friends at school. As he began counseling in a public service facility, he made new friends there. Alan had friends at church and friends in the neighborhood. He still has friends in the car circles, and his car still gives him satisfaction, but a sudden change in direction, which introduced him to new friends, helped Alan to avoid being consumed by his hobby at a time in his life when he was looking for fulfillment.

How are your friends influencing your life? Do they feed your addictive behaviors? Is it time you made new friends? My grandfather used to say, "If you're gonna' change, you're gonna' have to change your horses' watering hole." Maybe it's time for you to find a new "watering hole."

Chapter 14

How Can You Evaluate Your Friends?

It often seems when we are in the middle of a problem we have trouble seeing beyond that point. We become nearsighted and are only able to see what surrounds us. This may be the case with your friends. They are your friends and they are all you have. If you never had any different kinds of friends, it may be hard for you to tell whether the ones you now have are good for you or are simply contributing to your problems.

To expand your vision and give you a yardstick for measuring your personal situation, study the following characteristics of a healthy friendship. Think about your friends. Where do they fit into your life?

A true friend will allow you to be yourself. The recent deluge of material on the subject of co-dependency has made many of us afraid to share our needs and concerns with others for fear of being labeled "co-dependent." While these co-dependency concerns are real, they have been blown out of proportion.

Deborah was facing several very difficult situations in her life. Her ex-husband was fighting for custody of their children, she was starting a new job, and her boyfriend had just suggested they stop seeing each other for a while. Deborah felt that her entire life was falling apart. She needed someone to talk to, so she called her friend. But instead of allowing Deborah to be herself and to cry under the burden of her difficulties, her friend told her she needed to be strong and not so co-dependent. Now Deborah feels as though she needs to guard everything she says to this friend, lest she be criticized for her thoughts or actions.

Proverbs 17:17 says, "A friend loveth at all times" (KJV). In our good times and our bad times, a true friend will allow us to be ourselves.

A true friend will be open and honest. Jennifer came to Alpha Counseling through a friend. Her weight had gone up and down like a yo-yo, and she felt depressed all the time. As a result she was no longer the fun person she used to be, yet her friend hung in with her. When she could no longer cheer Jennifer up, her friend was honest with her and told her she needed professional help.

Emerson said, "The highest compact we can make with our fellow is—Let there be truth between us forevermore."

Because of her friend's honesty, Jennifer got help. You may recall from what I told you about her situation in chapter 5 that she found the source of her addiction to food, and after a time of treatment, she was able to return to a normal life.

Proverbs 12:17 says, "A good man is known by his truthfulness" (TLB). A true friend will be honest and open.

A true friend will show compassion. Lynn had been in counseling for a few months and was beginning to get in touch with the incest that haunted her adult behaviors. It was difficult for her to face the reality of her father's actions. After her therapy, Lynn felt wiped out and exhausted. She was fortunate to have an understanding husband who stood by her during this tough time. But Lynn hated to constantly dump her burdens on him. It seemed like they had so little time together, and she didn't want it all to be taken up discussing her problems. Yet she did need someone who cared. Her next-door neighbor Dawn was just the right person.

Dawn and Lynn made plans to go for walks on a regular basis. Because of their hectic schedules, their plans were often interrupted, but they were usually able to walk at least once a week. During these times, Lynn told Dawn what she was facing, and together they cried and prayed through the difficulties.

Luke 10:25-37 is the familiar story of the good Samaritan. In this story, a man was passing by on the road and saw another man in pain. Although he was not obligated to show compassion, the good Samaritan stopped and helped the wounded man. At the completion of the story, Jesus said, "Now go and do the same" (TLB). A true friend will show compassion for our needs. Compassion is a combination of love, care, and a desire to help.

A true friend is relaxed and makes you feel relaxed. Recently I went out to dinner with a group of friends—three couples. When we arrived at the restaurant, there were several empty tables around us, but other groups of people were seated nearby. The group I was with began talking, and soon we were sharing concerns about work, friends, and family. We told funny stories and exchanged vacation dreams. We laughed so hard that our sides hurt. When our check came, I noticed that two of the parties that came in after we did had already left. I don't know whether our noise chased them away or if we were just having so much fun that we failed to realize how quickly the time had passed. The point is that we were able to relax, be ourselves, and have a good time.

Throughout my years of counseling I have found that many people don't have anyone in their lives with whom they feel they can relax. They are like the city of Jerusalem in Lamentations 1:2: "She cries loudly at night. Tears are on her cheeks. There is no one to comfort her. All her lovers are gone. All of her friends have turned against her. They have become her enemies" (The Everyday Bible, New Century Version). A true friend will be there, let you be yourself, and allow you to drop your guard and relax.

A true friend can give and receive without being one-sided. Cheryl arrived in church ready to burst into tears. She was a few minutes late, and the little church was surprisingly full. Those whom she considered her friends had no empty seats near them. A sense of panic engulfed her as she scanned the room to find a place to sit. One of the elders spotted her and encouraged her to sit next to him and his wife.

The elder and his wife seemed to have it all together. They were happily married, and they had a nice house, good jobs, beautiful clothes, and fancy cars. Cheryl knew she would never have anything in common with these people, and here she was in her most volatile state. Her life was a series of mistakes. An adult child of divorce, she had also been sexually abused as a child. Her husband had beaten her, and she continued to be attracted to unhealthy relationships. With all her insecurities, Cheryl was sure this couple would want nothing of her.

However, her fears proved groundless. As Cheryl slipped into the seat, she said under her breath, "I feel like I am going to burst into tears." Laura smiled and encouraged her to sing along and take her mind off her problems. She pulled some tissue out of her purse and offered it to Cheryl. Cheryl dabbed at her eyes and tried to smile. Throughout the prayer time, Laura put her arm around Cheryl and hugged her. Cheryl's tears turned to sobs, and Laura suggested that they go into one of the smaller rooms.

As Cheryl shared her difficulties, she and Laura cried together. Laura told Cheryl about the tough year she'd just been through and the counseling that had helped her see beyond her own problems. Cheryl learned that she wasn't alone, that others had problems too. Laura could give Cheryl support and encouragement, and in turn, Cheryl could relate to Laura's situation. Together they could lift one another up. The relationship wasn't one-sided.

John 15:13 says, "Here is how to measure it—the greatest love is shown when a person lays down his life for his friends" (TLB). While few of us will truly be called to lay down our life, a true friend will lay down the wall of protection behind which hides his secrets and share in a friendship that involves give and take on both sides.

A true friend shows respect. Respect has been defined as "esteem for, a sense of the worth or excellence of, a person, a personal quality or trait, or something considered as a manifestation of a personal quality or trait." In other words, it is an attitude of high regard. In the biblical story of Saul and David, Saul was trying to kill David, yet David had an attitude of high regard for Saul as God's chosen king (see 1 Samuel 26:7-25).

Christians should show that kind of respect to one another. When you spend time with a true friend, you should be left feeling special and cared for.

A true friend will be an encourager. In 1 Samuel 23:17 we see how a true friend will encourage us: "Don't be afraid," Jonathan assured David. "My father will never find you! You are going to be the king of Israel and I will be next to you, as my father is well aware" (TLB). Jonathan was a true friend. He showed compassion for David by sharing his concerns and comforting him. Then he spoke words of encouragement to David by reminding him of his destiny.

While most of us can't be encouraged by a pending kingship, a true friend will give us encouraging words that are as fitting to our particular situation as Jonathan's words were to David.

Quentin had a friend named Tom. They had been friends for

years, and while their lives had taken different directions, they had continued to stay in touch. One preferred outdoor activities, and the other spent his spare time with books and intellectual pursuits. Every few months Quentin and Tom met at a restaurant. As Quentin shared with Tom the things he was doing and his accomplishments in life, Tom frequently scowled and asked, "Why would you want to do that?" He never got enthused over any of Quentin's projects or ideas.

As time passed, Quentin could see that he and Tom had become acquaintances rather than friends. He never heard an encouraging word from Tom, and as a result, their occasional meetings became perfunctory. Their relationship was no longer real.

A true friend is faithful and trustworthy. As we have seen, a true friend is someone with whom you can share both the good times and the bad times. Part of the ability to share what is on one's heart comes from the knowledge that the things which are shared will be kept in confidence. Proverbs 12:23 says, "A wise person keeps what he knows to himself" (The Everyday Bible, New Century Version). If our friends are healthy for us, they will be trustworthy.

God made us to be relational beings. The many Bible texts I've shared with you about friendship make that clear. We are supposed to have friends, but some friendships do more harm than good.

Now that you have a standard by which you can measure those with whom you associate, take some time to evaluate them. Ask yourself whether they are the kind of friends who may ruin you, or if they are there to help you.

Start by making a list of all your friends—the people outside your family whom you spend time with more than twice a month. Now get as many pieces of paper as you have names on your list. Put one name at the top of each piece of paper and begin writing the answers to the following questions on each person's page.

1. What do I receive from this person?
2. What does he or she receive from me?
3. How does this friend make me feel when we are together?
4. What does the relationship cost me in energy, dollars, and our effect on each other?

When you have completed this exercise, it should be clear to you how the relationships in your life measure up. You will know whether they are based on a mutual sharing and give and take, or if one of you does all the giving and receives nothing in return. You will be able to see which of your friends are trustworthy and faithful. Spending time with a friend should make you feel special and help you have a positive outlook on life.

Let's review the characteristics of a healthy friendship. First, a true friend will allow you to be yourself. If you feel that you need to change something about yourself when you are with this person or that you must put on airs, he or she is not truly your friend.

A true friendship is based on honesty. If you feel you can't truly share what is on your heart with this person, his or her friendship isn't helping you.

A true friend shows compassion. You can call him in a time of need, knowing that he will be there for you and will be glad to get involved in your life.

A true friend is relaxed with you and makes you feel relaxed. When you can take your shoes off, kick back, relax, and just have a good time together without any predisposed expectations, you have a true friend.

A true friend can give and receive. When the relationship is real and comfortable, friends share their hopes and dreams, hurts and difficulties with one another.

A true friend shows respect. When you are with this person, you will feel as though you are important to her. You will feel valued.

A true friend is an encourager. If you have an idea, he helps you develop it. If you've had a bad day, she will lift you up.

A true friend is faithful and trustworthy. When you share a secret, you can rest in confidence, knowing it will go no farther.

Any friend who meets these guidelines is a true friend. Open up to him. Make this person a part of your life, and let him help you on your road to healing. If he or she doesn't measure up, it may be time to join a support group and make some new friends.

Chapter 15

Why Do You Need a Support Group?

Once you have reviewed those within your circle of influence and begun to discontinue relationships you've had in the past with those who hold an unhealthy influence over you, it is important to rebuild your personal network of friends. If you do not systematically work at creating a healthy support system for yourself, loneliness will creep into your life and may cause you to make poor choices again just to have the companionship you miss.

Rebuilding a healthy support system for yourself and easing the loneliness are both important reasons why you need to be involved in a support group. Sarah found herself at church every time the doors were open. She became involved with every committee and every task. She was rewarded for her diligence, her sacrifice, and her hard work. People loved her and accepted her. She felt safe. Her church work became so all-consuming that she hardly had time for her job. Several times her boss caught her making copies of things for church on the company copier. She did phoning for the telephone committee when she thought no one was watching. Someone was. She got fired.

How could God do this to her? She was so good! Surely the people at church couldn't be "bad friends." But they were. She did the previous exercise to evaluate her friends and found that she was doing all the giving. Sarah had to stop attending that church in order to remove herself from these friends, but now she felt all alone, so she began attending a new church. Because of her loneliness, she was attracted to all the various activities the new church offered. However, she was aware of her tendency to bury herself in church projects to ease her poor self-esteem, and she realized that she was heading toward the same situation again. It's not that church activities are inherently wrong, but for Sarah they were an unhealthy way of filling a need in her life.

She needed someone who understood her dilemma. What a help it was when she became part of the support group her therapist was having. In the support group, she found others who also were struggling with unhealthy relationships and were working to break them. In the support group she made new friends who were understanding of each other's needs. They felt a true concern to help each other.

The support group provided Sarah with the kind of friendship she needed. It also created a system of accountability. Each week the members of the group shared how they were progressing and where they felt they were still having difficulties. They made commitments to work on certain areas of their lives, and together they checked with each other on the progress they were making in the predesignated areas.

Everyone in the group agreed that Sarah needed to broaden her network of friends to include a variety of people with varied interests. This would reduce the temptation to hide her hurts in church work. The accountability came each week as the group met. Sarah shared with the others what she had done the previous week to expand her world. She continued to attend church, but limited her involvement to one evening activity and the worship service on Sunday morning.

Sarah also made friends at her new job and began doing social things with them. One week she went to a Tupperware party, and everyone in her support group applauded her efforts at branching out. Another week she signed up for a class in desktop publishing to increase her computer skills. The support group kept Sarah accountable for accomplishing her goals.

While Sarah's support group met regularly, with a therapist in charge, the group doesn't have to be that structured to be effective. A church that understands the dynamics of interpersonal relationships can be an invaluable support group.

Henry and his wife were new at my church, and he made friends with many of the men through the monthly breakfast. We were all surprised to learn one day he had separated from his wife. He'd been having an affair with a younger woman and decided to move in with her. Those of us who had become his friends talked with his wife and learned that this was not the first time Henry had been unfaithful. Infidelity had been a recurring pattern in his life.

The men had already become a support system for Henry before he moved in with the other woman, so they confronted him. Several men from the church spent time with him, and within a few weeks Henry was able to cut himself free of the affair. He and his wife were reunited. While they have a long road together to heal the hurt that Henry's history of infidelity has created, they have the support of a church family that holds them accountable to their therapy program and appropriate behavior.

Support groups also provide a sense of community that helps in setting boundaries. Because of the abusive treatment Dana experienced as a child, she continually found herself in relationships with men who were emotionally or physically abusive. She was addicted to unhealthy relationships, and whenever she dated a man who was loving and gentle to her, she found him unattractive.

Her friends suggested that she take a women's assertiveness-training class at the local community college. She followed their suggestion and soon found she had the support of both the instructor and the other women in the class. The women learned to set boundaries in their relationships. Where the men in Dana's life had previously dominated her activities, the group helped her see that she could control her life. They told her how to respond if her boyfriend came to her house unannounced and uninvited.

She learned to tell him that he must call to see if she was available before stopping by. If the relationship became abusive, she learned to tell him to stop and to leave if the behavior persisted. With the help of the others in her class, Dana was able to regain control of her life, and once she no longer tolerated the abusive behaviors, her inappropriate suitors moved on to other relationships. As Dana got stronger, she found herself attracted to men she would have shunned before—men who treated her with respect and honor.

Your support group may be more of a care group that meets informally, without structure, to help those with similar needs to cope with their difficulties.

Nancy was molested by an uncle when she was a child. She had been in one structured support group and found it to be very helpful in her growth. Unfortunately, the government program that provided funding for the group's leadership ended. Without a leader or a place to meet, the group disbanded.

For a while Nancy didn't attend any group session. But she began to miss the fellowship and accountability the group had provided. When she heard about a nearby church that had several groups meeting on Tuesday night, Nancy signed up.

She attended for several weeks and found that the others in the group, including the leader, were just beginning their recovery process. Since Nancy had been involved in both a support group and individual therapy for some time, she found the others looking to her for answers. One evening after the group had completed the specified agenda and dismissed, several of the others stayed and asked her questions. While Nancy discovered that helping the others was rewarding and helpful to her overall recovery, she wasn't getting the support with her own problems that she needed.

When the group took a break for the holidays, Nancy didn't sign back up because the group wasn't supporting her. But she still missed what her earlier group had provided.

Nancy had several friends at work and at her church who were dealing with needs similar to hers. One of her friends had had an experience much like Nancy's with a support group. Others weren't currently involved in any type of support. As Nancy discussed these needs with several of the women, she found a common desire to be in a group.

Nancy's office had a spare room that could be used in the evening, and she decided to invite the others to an informal support session. Before the first session she read a few books on leading small groups so that she could structure her group to achieve healthy goals. While the makeup of the group varied from week to week, depending on people's individual schedules, there were generally six to eight women present.

Nancy acted as the leader in that she had organized the group, but the sessions were informal and consisted mostly of sharing and praying for one another. Different ones suggested books they had found helpful. They also shared appropriate scriptures, and together they grew through their problems. The women in this care group became like family to one another, and they lifted each other up at difficult times such as birthdays and holidays.

Nancy's family lived on the other side of the country, and she had typically flown home for Christmas. As Christmas approached, she began to feel depressed. Because of her changing jobs she couldn't afford to fly home, and she didn't have enough vacation time built up to make the trip worthwhile anyway. She would have to spend the holiday alone.

Fortunately, Kathryn, one of the other women in the group, was also going to be without her family for the first time and was also facing a difficult day. Kathryn was married and lived with her children in a house nearby, but she didn't like to cook. Nancy loved to cook. As they shared their mutual depression over the holiday with the group, they decided to get together. They planned the menu and shopped together.

When Christmas came, Nancy, Kathryn, and Kathryn's husband and children all went to the Christmas-eve service at Nancy's church. Afterward Nancy spent the night at Kathryn's house, and in the morning she cooked fresh buttermilk pancakes for her surrogate family. Later in the day she and Kathryn prepared the dinner, and all of them started a new tradition. Nancy had found herself a new family through her care group, and Kathryn had her traditional Christmas dinner even without her mom to cook it.

A support group can provide you with a surrogate or extended family. You may even find the "brother" or "sister" you never had. Whichever type of group you become a part of—whether an organized group with a trained leader, a church family, or a more informal care group—a support group can be there for you and provide emotional and spiritual growth.

Chapter 16

What Support Group Is Best for You?

Nancy has been involved in several different types of support groups. Her first group met with a counselor and focused directly on the issues that concern sexual-abuse victims. That group had been very helpful to Nancy's healing process. When this group was discontinued, Nancy joined a group led by a volunteer with little or no small-group experience. Now she realized how much the first group had helped her. While some of the women in the new group seemed to be helped by the weekly get-togethers, Nancy felt that the new group wasn't meeting her needs.

Like Nancy, you may have been involved in some support groups that met your needs and others that did not. A group that isn't meeting your needs may be good for others. Each of us brings to a group a different situation, and we each have our own expectations. If you have never been involved in a support group, you may find that almost any group is better than none at all. On the other hand, if you have been part of a group that fit your needs perfectly, your standards are likely to be higher, making it harder for you to find another group that meets your needs quite as well.

Also, each of us progresses at a different rate toward maturity, and a group that meets our needs at one level of growth may hold us back at a different level. For instance, if in addition to attending a support group you are getting counseling, reading books, and attending seminars, while others are only attending the group, you will grow at a faster pace than they do and sooner or later will very likely outgrow that group's ability to help you.

Just as different churches can meet the needs of different people, depending on the types of ministry each one offers, so different support groups can meet the needs of different people. A church takes on the personality of the people who gather there. The leader is particularly influential in determining the congregation's ministry. If the pastor focuses on outreach, the whole church will very likely have a welcoming flavor. If the leadership is strongly into mission work, that will be reflected in the activities of the church and the interest of the congregation. Some churches have a heavy emphasis on personal growth and offer classes and seminars to help the members, while others avoid anything they perceive to be humanism.

So it is with support groups. The personality or direction of a group is a combination of the people who attend the group and the leader's goals and agenda. When selecting a church that fits your needs and place in life, you usually must attend several services before making a decision. With support groups, you will also need to participate for a while to sense the flavor of the group and determine if it is the best place for you.

There are several things you can do to determine which groups will be best suited to your needs. If you are already involved in a support group, you can use these same guidelines to determine if your group is still meeting your needs.

Does the group provide emotional support? Start your evaluation by asking yourself if the group provides you with emotional support that allows you to deal with your thoughts, concerns, and feelings.

Pam didn't cope too well. For her, almost everything was a crisis, and her way of dealing with a crisis was to eat. She had tried every diet known to the human race. She'd lose weight and keep it off for a while, until the next crisis. It seemed that each crisis added more weight than the previous diet took off. Diets didn't work and fasting didn't work. She was fat and miserable. Eating made her feel good until she looked in the mirror. Pam finally faced the fact that she needed help.

A local civic group advertised a support group for people with eating disorders. One evening she got up the courage and went. There seemed to be no one in charge. A willowy little woman said this was not a seminar, just a discussion group—a chance to talk about mutual problems. She would get them started, the little woman said, and then she would leave.

It didn't take long for Pam to realize that this group was headed in a direction that she couldn't relate to. Most of the people were thin, and Pam found out that their problems involved a different eating disorder from the one she was experiencing. Most of them suffered with anorexia or bulimia and couldn't understand the frustration she felt over her constant weight gains. Pam was unable to provide the others with much support either, because she couldn't connect with their situations.

Pam felt depressed and confused. She stopped on the way home for ice cream and cried herself to sleep, thinking the next week would be better. It wasn't. It never got better. In addition to the fact that it was the wrong kind of group for her needs, the group had no direction and no purpose.

Does it get me in touch with my feelings? As we have discussed in previous chapters, addictive behaviors don't just appear from nowhere. They are usually a result of previous hurts or needs in our lives. As you are on the journey to healing your life, it is important for a support group to provide you with both support and growth. Ask yourself, "Does my group get me in touch with painful feelings from my past?"

As others in the group relate their stories and situations, their emotions will trigger memories from your own life. Often one member of the group will share something that will evoke a reaction in your mind. You may suddenly feel fear, anger, or hurt. You may be brought to tears by something that doesn't touch the others in the least. It is healthy to let these feelings come to the surface. Make note of experiences that touched you but were not shared by others in the group. Then share your feelings with the group. With their support you can look at your life and continue to learn more about your own background and the incidents that have set up your addictive behaviors.

One of the reasons to be part of a support group is hearing the stories of others who have been through similar experiences, because those stories will help you get in touch with the painful parts of your past.

Do I feel free to share? For a group to be right for you, you must feel free to share the difficult feelings you experience. So ask yourself, "Do

I feel free to share both good and bad things about myself and my life and express the emotions I am feeling?"

Gretchen came to Alpha Care Center, our in-patient treatment facility for women. She had been in another mental-health facility in our area and had been part of a structured support group while she was there. We encouraged her to express her feelings, but she had a hard time understanding that it was all right to really open up. Our therapist continued working with her, and in due time we found out that she had previously been advised not to allow all her feelings out. The doctors in the previous setting were afraid she might uncover something they wouldn't have time to deal with.

A group should allow you to share freely. One of the benefits of being in a structured group with a trained therapist is that if you do uncover extreme feelings, the therapist will know how to help you.

If the others in the group are judgmental or not supportive, you will not be comfortable sharing whatever is on your heart. Or, if most of the others in the group are farther along in their growth than you are, you may be afraid to open up for fear of looking foolish.

If the group fits you well, your growth and that of the other participants will be about the same, allowing each one to share both the good and the bad things he or she is feeling.

Am I growing? Another important aspect of the group experience is personal growth. If the group is good for you, you will continue to grow and progress. You will be a better and healthier person because you are part of the group. You may have a hard time determining how you are doing, but those who care about you will comment on your progress. This is important feedback.

Your growth can be compared to that of a small child. When you are with that child every day, his accomplishments seem less noteworthy. Because his progress takes place slowly, a little every day, it is easy to overlook how much he really has grown even in just a few weeks. But if you only see the child every few months, the changes will seem remarkable. You look at him and wonder how he grew so fast.

It's the same when you look at yourself. You may be growing beyond your addictive behaviors quite well but may find it hard to tell whether you are making progress because you see yourself every day. Others can see how far you have come much more easily.

Often, the people in your group will notice that your reactions have changed and improved much sooner than you do. Friends and family members who are concerned and aware of your struggles will also be able to confirm whether you are making progress.

So don't be discouraged if you are not moving along as fast as you think you should. Check with those who are involved in your life. If they see improvement, the group is probably playing a part in helping to make you a better person even if at times it doesn't seem so.

Do I miss the group when I can't attend? Last, ask yourself, "If I can't attend a session, do I miss it?" Rhonda had been forcing herself to attend a support group because her friends had suggested it might help her deal with some problems in her life. One week she had to go out of town on business with her husband. When the time came for the group to start back at home, Rhonda felt a great sense of relief that she wasn't there. She didn't miss it at all! Rhonda realized that the group had become a drag to her. The fact that she didn't miss the group helped her to know that it wasn't the right place for her to be anymore.

As you evaluate the group you have been part of, be sure to look at all five of these factors, and give the group time. Two or three sessions is not a sufficient time frame to know whether a group is right for you. Groups tend to go through stages. Marianne Schneider Corey and Gerald Corey are experts at leading groups of various kinds. In their book *Groups, Process and Practice*, the Coreys mention six stages by which they evaluate a group: Pregroup, initial, transition, working, final, and postgroup stages. There are three natural stages a group will go through before it gets to the point where it becomes a working group.

The pregroup stage is the time when the criteria for the group's composition is being determined. This is the stage when the members are getting acquainted with one another and learning what is expected of them. In the transition stage the group members are testing the leader and each other to determine how safe the environment is. In the working stage the level of trust and cohesion is high. Communication is open, and people feel comfortable expressing their true feelings. It is in the working stage that you can best make an assessment of the group's relationship to your needs.

A group should move no faster than one phase per meeting. So to properly evaluate the group's value to you, you will need to attend for several sessions.

Whether the group you are part of is a formal group, with a trained therapist as the leader; a Bible-study group; or a care group, a good support group will always provide a ground level of love and support that will be there for you regardless of what you do. How is your support group? Is it meeting your needs?

Chapter 17

Do You Have Blind Spots?

As your healing process moves along, you may feel tempted to think that you've improved so much you can stop working on your problem. While you may be much better and much happier than you were before you started on this journey, you still may not be home free. Now is the time to stop and evaluate the progress you have made, and also to identify areas that still need work. With each addictive behavior you deal with, you will usually discover other problems that are a result of the prior abuse or a byproduct of the present addiction.

Jim had a blind spot in his life that was a result of his prior abuse. He had made great progress in overcoming his addiction to food. He had come a long way with counseling, the right friends, and an eating-disorders support group. He had attained many of the goals he had set for himself at the beginning of his journey. He had lost weight, his marriage was improving, and his professional life was looking brighter. Because he had made such excellent progress, Jim wanted to quit his therapy. He failed to see the areas that were still struggles for him.

The root issue that had caused an eating problem for Jim was childhood abuse. His father had no tolerance for mistakes. His father was a large, violent man. Even his mother was afraid to stand up to him, and they finally separated. After Jim's father left, his mother tried to comfort him by offering him treats such as cookies or ice cream.

Thus Jim learned to dull his emotional pain by eating—a pattern that became a severe problem in his adult life. Instead of dealing with the difficulties that came up, he dulled the pain with food. However, with therapy and group counseling he was able to lose weight and correct many of his behaviors.

While the obvious problem had been corrected, there were still blind spots of which Jim was unaware. As a result of his childhood abuse, Jim had always overreacted to his children's misbehavior. While his eating was getting under control, he was still close to being violent with his own children. He had learned his parenting skills the same way most of us do—by watching his parents. His father reacted violently to misbehavior, and so did he. Since this parenting style was all he knew, he couldn't see that it needed correction. Jim thought he was better—and he was, but there were still troubled areas in his life that he didn't see. He needed the help of an objective advisor.

Through Jim's healing journey, communication between him and his wife had improved. They frequently saw the counselor together. Jim's wife had tried to bring up his behavior toward the children, but Jim had always reacted with denial. In one of their sessions together, his wife addressed the subject again. Now that he had cleared up many of the other issues in his life, Jim was able to accept the fact that there were other areas that still needed work. The counselor helped him to understand that his violent behavior was inappropriate.

Blind spots may also be a result of the addictive behaviors themselves. In the case of a shopping addiction, a black cloud of debt usually hangs around even after the compulsive behavior has been corrected. The debt creates its own problems. Since most shopping addicts shop to boost their self-esteem, the progress they have made on their journey toward healing can be thwarted by the debt blind spot.

It happened just that way with Virginia. Her husband had left her for a younger woman. She felt unattractive and undesirable. To give herself a fresh outlook on life, she took advantage of a makeover session offered by a local department store. She had her hair styled and bought all the new cosmetics. She liked her new look, and she felt much better about herself, but her old clothes seemed inappropriate for her youthful new image. She shopped some more. Over the months, as she adjusted to her loss, she became quite a shopper.

In counseling, Virginia did many of the exercises outlined in this book. She overcame her low self-esteem and even started dating. She no longer shopped just for the sake of shopping. But she still had outstanding balances on most of her credit cards that she was unable to pay off.

Virginia felt that she was fully healed and ready to discontinue her counseling, but as the bill collectors called, she began to feel worthless again. She refused to return their calls, which added to the problem. She was blind to what she was doing. As we discussed how the calls made her feel, she was able to see that she needed to design a plan for repayment. Once she made contact with her creditors and began making monthly payments that she could afford, they stopped calling.

Jim and Virginia both defended their egos with the feeling that because they had made progress they didn't need any more help. While we all have a natural desire to do well, we often impede our progress by patting ourselves on the back too soon. Our subconscious mind uses our blind spots to protect us from the temporary discomfort that dealing with our issues causes.

Jim didn't want to look any farther than his weight problem. Although it was painful to admit how his violence was affecting his children, doing so allowed him to complete the healing process.

Virginia wanted to ignore the creditors' calls. She was embarrassed to have to tell them she couldn't pay her bills. But painful as the experience was, swallowing her pride and making the needed adjustments in her payment schedule allowed her to keep on growing.

Think about your life. What areas may still be blind spots for you? It is difficult to identify a blind spot yourself, but there are several indicators that will help point you in the right direction.

Overreaction is usually a red flag. We discussed the case of Randy and Terese. Randy overreacted when Terese left him, which indicated that there were deeper issues he had not yet dealt with. We overreact to situations because we have unprocessed pain from similar situations in our past that "fuel" our present issues. It's easy to spot this problem in others around us, but more imortant that we see it in ourselves. It provides a clue to our areas of emotional need.

Discomfort is another indication. Virginia didn't want to return the calls to the bill collectors because it was painful to face her financial instability. This discomfort was a clue to an area that needed additional work. Because addictions always mask pain of some type, discomfort and pain are the "fuel" that feeds addictions. You should also watch for the discomfort of others. If many people react uncomfortably or bring up an area of concern repeatedly, don't write them off. God may be using their concerns to shed light on your life.

In chapter 19 we will discuss the value of having someone from whom you can accept critique and feedback. That objective person can help you see any blind spots that may still be left in your life.

Chapter 18

How Do You Measure Progress?

If you have ever traveled with children, you know that before you have been on the road an hour, they'll be asking, "Are we there yet?"

Most of us respond to the healing journey in much the same way. We get started, pass a few landmarks, read a book or two, and we think we should be there. But healing takes time. We may be tired of the trip and think we must surely be there by now, but there is still a way to go.

I had a motorcycle when my wife Carol and I were still young and newly married. On weekends we used to enjoy going for a ride in the mountains surrounding the Los Angeles area. One day we decided to visit a beautiful spot called Crystal Lake, which is nestled high up in the hills. The road rises from about sea level to almost 4,500 feet above in just a few miles, giving you the feeling that you are traveling straight up!

We had made many mountain journeys, but this was one of the steepest climbs we had ever taken, and the motorcycle got very hot under the strain. Feeling the heat on my legs, I pulled off to the side to let the motorcycle rest, and while it was resting, Carol and I took a little walk around the curve ahead. I remember thinking, as I looked up at the rock cliffs, "We'll never make it. That is too far to go." But walking back to the motorcycle we looked over the edge of the road to the curves below us and were awestruck at how far we had come.

Looking at the distance we had already covered gave us confidence that we could finish the comparatively short distance to the top. We did make it all the way to Crystal Lake, and when we got there we discovered it was beautiful. We agreed it was well worth the trip even though we had had to stop from time to time for rest.

That's how it is with your healing journey. While the road ahead may look steep, when you look at how far you've come, you can see your progress and receive encouragement for the rest of the trip. You may need to stop and rest from time to time, and that's OK. The road may get too steep in places for you to forge ahead without a breather. But, as soon as you are ready, get back on your mental motorcycle and keep going.

I believe it is Satan's wish that we stay disabled. When we've made good progress, he works extra hard to knock us down and make us believe that we can't change, that we are stuck living with our problems.

Remember Nancy—the woman who started an evening care group? She had been in therapy for several years and had made tremendous progress. She was making healthy decisions. She had changed jobs and had a wonderful support system of friends and colleagues. She was helping others and knew that what she was doing was making a difference in her life. One day Nancy stopped for a breather, looked back at where she had been just one year earlier, and was amazed at how much better she was responding to life. Yes, she had come a long way in her healing journey.

But then something happened that shook her up. She got a call from her mother. The uncle who had molested her when she was younger had been sick and had just died. While Nancy had no fond feelings toward her uncle, the news of his death brought back a flood of emotions. The tears and the sickness in her stomach surprised her. She thought she had dealt with the molestation and its surrounding issues, but now, at the mention of her uncle's name, she was a mess all over again.

One day at work Nancy got a call from one of the women who was part of her support group. The woman wanted Nancy to drop by that evening and discuss some of her problems. She needed Nancy's help.

Nancy had come a long way, and she knew she needed to spend time alone to process the pain she was feeling. She wisely told her friend that she couldn't stop by that night. Unfortunately, the woman reacted with some rather hostile remarks.

After she hung up, Nancy began to feel guilty. She wondered

whatever made her feel like she knew enough or had come far enough to help someone else. Satan played games with her mind, making her feel like she'd wasted her time in counseling, that reading books was getting her nowhere, and that she should quit her group. The next time Nancy came in for counseling, we worked on the following exercise to help her see how far she had really come. She was encouraged with her progress and was able to see that the hurtful comments the woman in her group had made were out of her own need and not intended to hurt Nancy.

When you begin to feel like it's not worth it all and you want to quit, it's time to stop and take a look at how far you've come. After you have been on your journey of healing from an addiction for a while, stop and ask yourself the following questions. In addition to checking off the boxes provided, think over each question. If a specific story or example of your growth comes to mind, include it in your journal. You may find it helpful to review sections of your journal that you wrote six months to a year ago. Your comments and feelings back then will help you to evaluate how far you have come and how your reactions have changed.

Answer each of the following questions with a number from one to five, with one being poor and five being excellent:

____1. Are you getting along better with your friends and family?
     For your journal: If you can think of a recent incident when your response was different from what it would have been six months or a year ago, write what happened. Then write how you would have handled the same thing previously and how you handled it today.

____2. Are you feeling better physically?
     For your journal: Think back six months to a year. Did you frequently have headaches, stomach problems, a cold or the flu, or other stress-related aliments? What is the status of these problems today? Write in your journal how you felt then and compare that with how you feel today. Most people find that as they progress, the problems of life don't throw them as much, their stress is reduced, and therefore they feel better.

____3. Are you being more kind to yourself?
     For your journal: Last year, did you do anything that was just for

you? How did it make you feel? Have you learned to take better care of yourself? Write out your response to these questions and list some of the things you are doing today to meet your emotional, physical, and spiritual needs.

____4. Are you feeling closer to God?

For your journal: Write down how you felt about God a year ago. How do you feel about Him today? In what ways has your relationship with Him changed?

____5. Are you handling disappointments better?

For your journal: Think of some of the disappointments you faced last year. Write down what they were and how you responded. Then list some of the disappointments you have faced in the last week or two and jot down how you responded this time. Compare the two and take note of how you have or have not progressed.

____6. Do you have a better attitude about the things you cannot change?

For your journal: List the things in life that have bothered you but you could do nothing about—things like your parents' reactions, your appearance, or the growth of others who are close to you. Write down how you responded to these things last year and how you are responding this year. Are you responding or reacting better?

____7. Can you see the accomplishment of realistic goals?

For your journal: List the goals you set for yourself in the past. Did you achieve them? How did you feel when you did or did not achieve them? Are you still reaching for the same goals, or have you set new ones? If your goals are different today, list what they are and the progress you are making toward reaching them. How does this progress make you feel?

____8. Have your fears decreased?

For your journal: Think back six months to a year ago. Were you having dreams that made you fearful? Were you afraid to let others know how you were feeling? Were you afraid to go out of your house or afraid to stay home alone? List the things you used to be afraid of, and write down how you feel about those same things today. Is there a difference?

____9. How are people responding to you today?

For your journal: Write down how those who are close to you and knew about your personal struggles responded to you a year ago—the comments they made. Then write down the state of your emotional health and your reactions to life at that time. Have the comments by others changed in the last year? Ask some of those within your support system if they have seen any progress in you in the last year. Ask them for specifics and note their comments in your journal.

After you have completed this exercise, review both your numerical answers and your written comments. You may not see a major improvement in every area of your life, but you should be able to see a pattern of growth in many areas. While each person's growth will be different because of varying conditions, such as the nature of the addictive behavior, counseling, the amount of time available for reading, and each one's support system, you should notice some improvement within each six-month period of your life. Keep checking your growth by going through this exercise about every six months.

Growth is a journey. Rather than looking ahead at how far you have to go, look back at how much ground you have covered and how far you've come.

Chapter 19

Who Should Give Feedback?

In a previous chapter we discussed the importance of having objective feedback to help in measuring your progress. Galatians 6:1, 2 says that the input of others in our lives is important: "Brothers, someone in your group might do something wrong. You who are spiritual should go to him and help him make it right again. You should do this in a gentle way. But be careful! You might be tempted to sin, too! Help each other with your troubles. When you do this, you truly obey the law of Christ" (The Everyday Bible, New Century Version).

Many people may offer their opinions, but not everyone has a right to give you feedback, nor should you listen to every person who offers an opinion about your progress. Second Corinthians 10:12 says, "We dare not make ourselves of the number, or compare ourselves with some that commend themselves: but they measuring themselves by themselves, and comparing themselves among themselves, are not wise" (KJV). You need to reach outside of your closest circle of friends or family and get objective feedback from those whose thinking has not been damaged in the same area as yours or who have not been affected by your problems. The Bible says not to compare ourselves among ourselves.

A person who is too close to you, such as a spouse or parent, may not be far enough removed from the situation to give an objective opinion. You'll end up with what's called "comparing ourselves with ourselves."

Hershel came seeking help from his addiction to work. His wife Lee was at her wits' end and was threatening to leave him, which prompted his search for help. Lee was so close to the situation and so emotionally involved that she refused to be happy until Hershel was home *early* every night, not just on time. If a vital business meeting caused Hershel to miss a soccer game, even with advance notice, Lee was unhappy. So while Lee desperately wanted to see improvement in Hershel's addictive behavior, she was too close to be able to see how far he had really come. She would only be satisfied when he had completed the journey.

Sometimes family members can offer constructive feedback, but often this is difficult when the addiction directly affects them. Those who offer opinions need to be balanced themselves. If they are struggling with their own addictive behaviors, their thinking may be colored by where they are, which will make it difficult for them to be objective.

You will recall Cindy, who had become addicted to exercise. The more the addictive behavior progressed, the less she saw of her normal friends. Everyone she spent time with at the gym and in her spare time was equally involved in keeping fit. Since they were involved in the same activities as Cindy, they couldn't give objective advice about her emotional progress. As she got healthier and didn't need to be at the gym to build her self-worth, her friends actually thought she was going downhill. Her weight-lifting ability diminished while she was recuperating from her medical problems. They were unable to understand that a slight loss of strength was actually progress. Sometimes our friends can offer an objective opinion, but not when they are equally involved or unbalanced themselves.

The person who evaluates your progress should be someone who doesn't need anything from you. If your addictive behavior gives him or her a benefit, the opinion you get will be swayed by that person's own needs.

Sarah was the "salvation" of the church. She was involved in every committee and was a beloved Bible-study teacher, and the people at church were unhappy when she decided that she needed a change in order to overcome her addictive behavior. As long as she continued attending that church, everyone expected her to keep doing everything she had buried herself in before. She expected an objective response when she told the pastor that she was leaving and why. Instead he became angry with her. He told her that he was sure Satan was prompting her actions, because God wanted her to give herself sacrificially to the church. Many pastors can give objective feedback, but this can be difficult when your growth causes him and his church personal loss.

Those who offer objective feedback should not be so close to the problem that they cannot see your progress. They should have balance in their own lives, and they should have nothing to gain by your addictive behaviors. These are things to avoid in your search for feedback.

Let's look at what you *do* want in a person who can help you monitor your progress. First, the person whose advice you are seeking should exhibit the fruits of the Spirit in his or her life. While we are not called to judge the Christian experience of others, Galatians 5:22-26 offers us a guideline for determining those who live by the Spirit. They will have "love, joy, peace, patience, kindness, goodness, faithfulness, gentleness, self-control [and are] not . . . proud, [do] not make trouble with each other, [and are] not . . . jealous of each other" (The Everyday Bible, New Century Version). These are the qualities you need to look for as you seek objective feedback.

Your advisors should be people who know how to set healthy boundaries. When they have reached a point where they are not comfortable with your growth or progress, they will honestly tell you where you stand. If they do not feel equipped to offer advice, they will suggest someone else you can ask. This is especially true of a therapist or counselor. No human being has all the answers—not even those with extensive training. But a good counselor will have a network of associates he can refer you to for specialized assistance.

Chapter 20

How Long Will It Take?

You don't call it a journey, or even a trip, when you dash off to the grocery store to pick up a quart of milk. You typically expect to be gone a matter of minutes. You know the road you will take and which landmarks you will pass. You know where to turn to get to the store, and when you walk inside, you know exactly which aisle has the milk. There are no real mysteries.

If, on the other hand, you were to drive from one side of America to the other, you would encounter a lot of unknown territory. It would be a time-consuming journey. You would go many places you had never been, see landmarks you'd never seen, and experience things you'd never felt before. Rather than an everyday event, crossing America by car or motor home would be a journey. To prepare for the trip, you would read travel guides and talk to others who have been to the places you intend to visit.

As you talked with those who have made the journey before you, you would find that some crossed the country in record time. They drove straight through, didn't run into any traffic jams or mechanical problems, and were able to steer clear of the speed traps.

Others would have a totally different story. Some might have taken a less direct route to allow them to stop at various scenic landmarks. Others might have had a flat tire or an overheating problem along the way that slowed their progress, but as long as they kept going and didn't give up, those who went slower did eventually reach their destination.

Both groups reached the goal. But the route each person took was different, each one saw different things, and each has his or her own unique stories to tell. That's why, even though there are so many books about travel, each one can be true and factual. There are many right ways to cross America, and each person has a unique story of how he or she did it.

That's how it is with the journey from dysfunction to a functional way of life. Many have made the journey before you, and each one has his or her own stories to tell. Many of these stories have been chronicled in "travel guides"—books on addiction and co-dependency that tell you how to have a better life. Sometimes these books seem to contradict one another, but in reality they are different routes to the same goal. There is no one answer that works for each person.

As you prepare to make your journey toward wholeness, you will see that, just as with a physical journey, there are various stages that people go through; and while we can all reach the goal, there is no set formula that works exactly the same for everyone. Just as there are different vehicles with varying speed capabilities, so each person will travel at his or her own pace. Those who make the cross-country journey by themselves will have to stop for rest more often, while those who travel as a group will have a support team to trade off driving. Those who study and prepare prior to departure will have a better understanding of the route and will be better prepared for the roadblocks they may face. The traveler who headed off on an impulse may turn back at the first sign of difficulty.

There are so many variables to the journey to wholeness that it is impossible to predict an exact time frame for your trip. But like the physical journey, the better prepared you are and the more support you have, the sooner you will reach your destination.

While the timing is unpredictable, every traveler has the same parts of the journey to take. Understanding these parts and the potential time frames of each one will help you as you begin your trip.

The first part of your plan may have to be simply to gain an awareness of your need. That's where this book can help. As you read through *Too Much Is Never Enough*, you may have recognized certain addictive behaviors that you have used to keep you from feeling some of the pain from your past. This recognition is often a painful stage in itself. You may be in a situation like Hershel's. His wife's threat to leave forced him to look at his life. Or, like Randy, your spouse may have already left, leaving you with shattered hopes and dreams. Your story may be more like Cindy's, whose addictive behavior almost cost her her job. Whatever your story, and whichever addictive behaviors have been a part of your life, you may have to experience personal pain before you can recognize that you need to change.

Chapters 10, 11, and 12 are especially designed to help you recognize your addictive behaviors. As you plan your course, it is important that you know what you are recovering from. Read the books outlined for you in chapter 10, and read additional books by others who have already made the journey. Reading the stories of other travelers will help you plan and give you realistic expectations for the trip.

Chapter 14 includes an exercise that will help you to evaluate your friends. As you do that exercise, you may see that some of your friends have been a detriment to your spiritual and emotional growth, and you will decide to replace them with friends who can have a positive influence on your life. Friends who are a part of your old habit patterns will hinder your progress. Part of your planning must be to have friends who will cheer you on and lift you up.

You must have a support system in place before you start your journey. It may be a structured group, with a therapist as its leader. It may be a group of fellow travelers, some of whom are just starting out, while others will have made some progress down the road. Or your support system may be a strong and caring church family. Whatever support you have available, be sure the people are willing to be available when you need them. Like any journey, you are bound to hit obstacles, and having a support system that encourages you to keep going is essential.

Planning your course may only take a few weeks or even days. If you know your addictions, if your friends are with you, and you are part of a support system, much of your plan may already be made. The planning part of your recovery may be merely a matter of checking off your progress.

On the other hand, if you are having a hard time even admitting that you have addictive behaviors, if you haven't been reading about the recovery process, and your support system isn't in place, planning your course and getting everything ready for the trip could take a year or even longer.

Once you have completed your plans, you are ready to embark on your healing journey. The journey is simply a combination of the components presented in *Too Much Is Never Enough* that will help you to process the pain from your past. A typical journey is made up of counseling, group discussions, reading, and prayer. Because there are different kinds of counselors and group experiences, and because the amount of time individuals can commit to the journey will vary, each person's trip will be unique.

I have found that three things determine the length of time it takes for my clients to make this journey. One is defensiveness. As a result of the experiences that led up to the addictive behavior, and during the time it has had an effect on their life, many people develop defenses that help them to maintain their self-esteem. Unfortunately, these defenses tend to create a false sense of security that makes genuine healing more difficult. The more defensive a person is, the longer his or her journey will take. If you are willing to be open and honest with yourself and those who are supporting your efforts, you will make much more rapid progress.

A second factor that will affect the length of your journey is the amount of time you can commit to it. The more time you devote to it, the faster you will move along. If you were to take a trip across the United States and could drive straight through, you'd get there fast. Stopping to take care of the kids and carry on business would impede your progress. Those who have the luxury of both time and finances to take advantage of a twenty-four-hour, fully licensed acute facility like the Alpha Care Center can shorten their journey remarkably. Intensive care such as this allows you to deal with your issues twenty-four hours a day, seven days a week, without the interruption of daily responsibilities. However, most people have to continue filling their regular obligations, fitting their journey toward wholeness around the rest of their lives. Their journey will naturally take longer.

Last, as you journey toward wholeness, the better you get acquainted with yourself, the more quickly you will move along. If you measure your progress as discussed in chapter 18 and keep a journal, you will begin observing patterns about yourself. As you learn to know yourself better, you will circumvent or walk around the roadblocks that you encounter instead of letting them stop your progress.

Denise recently made a discovery about herself that removed one of her roadblocks. Each year she joined her husband on a business trip. Since he was part of a family business, this involved spending time with the in-laws. Denise's husband flew off to the meeting on Wednesday, and she joined him on Friday by driving there with her in-laws. Unfortunately, her in-laws changed their projected departure time several times the week before the trip. By looking at her journal from the previous year's trips, Denise saw that this was a pattern for them. She also realized that their "on-again, off-again" behavior caused her a great deal of stress.

Because she had already been on her healing journey for a year, Denise was getting to know herself better. She was able to anticipate her in-laws' behavior by packing on Wednesday. She was ready to leave anytime after that. When her mother-in-law called on Thursday to say that they were thinking of leaving Thursday night instead of Friday afternoon, Denise was flexible. Because she'd learned about herself and what areas were apt to "push her buttons," she could face the roadblock without a setback.

Your journey will progress more quickly if you are open and honest with yourself, make time to invest in the trip, and allow yourself to learn from your experiences. Your journey may require as little as six months, or it may take two years or even longer. Each person will take a different road to the same destination, and therefore each one's time on the journey will be different.

As you plan your journey, and then as you take your journey toward healing, you will find that from time to time you will need to correct your course. This involves changing behavior patterns. By the time we humans have reached adulthood, we have established certain ways of dealing with life's problems. If you are addicted, your addiction is part of your pattern. Changing these habit patterns is sometimes called "reprogramming of old tapes." It's as though all of us have tapes playing in our heads that tell us what to do and how to react. During the planning phase of your journey and during the early days of the journey itself, you will very likely find yourself reacting to problems the same way as before. The "old tapes" are still telling you what to do.

Throughout the course of a year, you will encounter a number of opportunities to change your tapes. During that time, you will live through a birthday, family holidays, a summer vacation, and other significant events in your life in which the "old tapes" typically control your behavior. However, by putting forth deliberate effort to play "new tapes," you can correct your course.

You can expect the phase of correcting your course to take a minimum of one year. However, as the saying goes, "Old habits die hard," so don't be disappointed if the changes take even longer.

Toward the end of your journey, you will be ready to review your course. As we discussed in chapter 18, you can review your progress, much like looking back over a map, to see how far you have traveled. By looking back over two or three years of efforts to recover, you will be able to see how much you have changed and grown.

Reviewing your course should actually be a lifelong process. Like a favorite trip from which you share stories with others for the rest of your life, reviewing your course is something you should do over and over again, both for yourself and the benefit of others who are just beginning their healing journey.

Chapter 21

How Can You Know When It's Over?

As you prepare to close the book on your addictive behaviors, you may be asking yourself, "How do I know if I am really healed?" or "Where do I go from here?"

While we are not directly addressing the issues of alcoholism in *Too Much Is Never Enough*, we can use it for some comparisons. Earlier in this book you read about my friend who was a teenage alcoholic. He no longer drinks, but he tells me that if he takes one drink, he will be addicted to alcohol again. Additionally, his lifestyle exhibits several other addictive behaviors. He isn't truly healed. He simply has the offensive behavior under control and has replaced it with more acceptable behaviors, such as frenetic activity, which keep him from having to face his pain.

Alcoholism is a chemical addiction, and it does have certain characteristics that are different from the psychological addictions we have discussed in *Too Much Is Never Enough*. But in the same way, having the offensive behaviors of a psychological addiction under control doesn't mean that you are healed.

You will know you are truly healed when you can be around your previously addictive behaviors and even participate in them without feeling an emotional or physical pull to make the activity an excessive part of your life. If your addictive behavior was in the area of sports, and the men of your church decide to go as a group to the big game being played between your local team and its arch rival, you should be able to enjoy yourself and go home without feeling like you ought to buy season tickets. Someone like Cindy, who was addicted to exercise, should be able to join a health club and keep in shape but set a reasonable limit on the amount of time invested in that particular activity.

Most men and women who have struggled with an addictive behavior and come through a healing process can engage in the activity that had been so soothing and wonder what was so enticing about it. Once you are truly healed, the addictive activity becomes just like any other in your life. You do it from time to time, but it no longer consumes you.

When you are truly healed, you will not feel like there is a hole in your life from the removal of your addictive behavior. As you begin to let go of your addiction, your life will take on more balance. Rather than being consumed by a single activity or two, you will lead a fulfilling life, with your time spent in a variety of activities. Your priorities will be in order. No one activity will stand between you and your relationship with God or keep you from your family responsibilities.

When you are truly healed, not only from the addictive behavior but from your need for the addiction, you will begin to notice others around you who are striving to cover their pain with some activity as you once were. Rather than judging them and placing yourself in a more "holy" position because you no longer struggle as they do, have compassion. Turn your healing into helping.

Once you are healed, you can share your story with others. The sharing could take place as part of a church service or in a Bible study. As you share, you may discover many others who are ready to embark on their own healing journey. You can help them by being there for them as a personal "tour guide," or lead several at a time through a class or support group. The book *Giving Back*, by Marita Littauer, suggests several ministry ideas, all with complete instruction, that can help you turn your healing into helping.

What do you do when the person you can't stand . . . is you?

Sometimes I Don't Like Myself is an intensely personal look into author Candace Schap's pursuit of a love and respect she feared would never be hers—and how she found it. With honesty and vulnerability she explores:

- reasons we suffer from poor self-esteem,
- how to identify the causes of insecurity, and
- the liberating discovery of God's unconditional love.

From the author of ***Sometimes I Don't Like My Kids*** comes vital counsel that will help you see yourself with new eyes—and like what you see.

US$7.95/Cdn$9.55. Paper.

Now available at your local Christian bookstore.

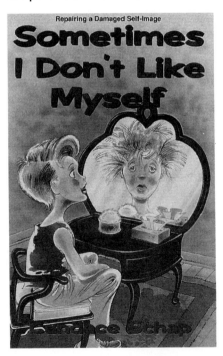

Repairing a Damaged Self-Image

Sometimes I Don't Like Myself

Candace Schap

New Devotional for Overeaters Who Crave the Power of God!

During Pauline's battle with overeating, she craved more than food. She desired God's acceptance and help in developing new thought patterns to achieve her goals.

A Table Before Me, by Pauline Ellis Cramer, blends anecdotes, words of wisdom, and Scripture into a wonderful little book of devotions that will help you walk with God through your own daily recovery program.

US$7.95/ Cdn$9.55. Paper.

Get it today at your local Christian bookstore.

© 1992 Pacific Press Publishing Association 2534b